THE COMPLETE MEDITERRANEAN DIET COOKBOOK FOR BEGINNERS

125 Affordable, Easy-to-Follow Recipes for No-Stress Weight
Management and Lifelong Wellness!
Includes Shopping List

TABLE of CONTENTS

Chapter 4
Veggies and Side Dishes 38

Chapter 5
Fish and Seafood 50

Chapter 6
Meat and Poultry 61

Chapter 7
Desserts 74

INTRODUCTION

Welcome to "**The Complete Mediterranean Diet Cookbook for Beginners**"—your guide to the simplicity, richness, and health benefits of Mediterranean eating. More than just recipes, it's a lifestyle rooted in tradition, balance, and the joy of wholesome foods. Whether you're new to this diet or looking to learn more, this cookbook will help you make it part of your daily life.

Inside, you'll find easy-to-follow recipes that capture the flavors and ingredients of the Mediterranean. From breakfasts to dinners, each dish fits effortlessly into your routine, providing nutrition and satisfaction. Designed for beginners, these recipes feature clear instructions and simple ingredients, making healthy cooking accessible to everyone.

Discover the essence of Mediterranean eating—a balance of vegetables, fruits, whole grains, healthy fats, and lean proteins. These recipes bring the Mediterranean lifestyle to your kitchen, allowing you to enjoy delicious flavors while supporting long-term wellness.

The Mediterranean diet's flexibility lets you cook with what you love. Use your favorite meats, fish, or plant-based proteins, add fresh vegetables and herbs, or modify ingredients to suit your taste. Make each dish your own, embracing the creativity that defines Mediterranean cooking.

My goal is to make this diet a joyful, lasting part of your life. With this cookbook, you'll find the inspiration to cook confidently, enjoy every bite, and benefit from this timeless way of eating. Welcome to a world of flavorful, nourishing food that will transform your daily meals.

Welcome to Mediterranean Cooking

Welcome to the vibrant world of Mediterranean cooking, where centuries of tradition and culture come together to create dishes that are both delicious and nourishing. The Mediterranean diet is more than just a way of eating; it's a lifestyle rooted in the ancient customs of countries bordering the Mediterranean Sea. From the olive groves of Greece to the markets of Italy and Spain, this diet reflects the rich agricultural heritage and culinary ingenuity of the region.

The origins of Mediterranean cooking date back thousands of years, grounded in simple, wholesome ingredients like olives, wheat, and grapes—staples that have stood the test of time. This diet gained international attention in the mid-20th century when researchers discovered that people in the Mediterranean had lower rates of heart disease and longer life expectancies. The secret? A focus on fresh, seasonal produce, healthy fats, and lean proteins, all prepared with minimal fuss.

Mediterranean cooking is not just about what you eat, but how you eat. Meals are enjoyed slowly, often with family and friends, celebrating the social aspect of food. Whether it's a simple meal of grilled fish and vegetables or a festive spread of mezze, Mediterranean cuisine invites you to savor the flavors and the moment. As you embark on this culinary journey, you'll discover that every dish tells a story, connecting you to a tradition of eating that has brought joy and health for generations. Welcome to the Mediterranean table, where food is life, and life is celebrated.

The Mediterranean Diet: A Journey to Improved Well-Being

The Mediterranean diet is more than just a way of eating—it's a journey toward better health and well-being. By focusing on whole foods like fruits, vegetables, whole grains, and healthy fats, this diet promotes heart health, longevity, and overall vitality. It's a lifestyle that encourages balance, moderation, and enjoyment, making it easy to sustain and highly rewarding.

Finding Joy in Simplicity: Where Efficiency and Contentment Meet

The Mediterranean diet embodies the joy of simplicity, where efficiency in meal preparation meets the contentment of enjoying wholesome, delicious food. With a focus on fresh, seasonal ingredients and straightforward cooking methods, this diet allows you to create nourishing meals with minimal effort, leaving more time to savor life's simple pleasures.

The Benefits of the Mediterranean Diet

The Mediterranean diet offers numerous health benefits, from improving heart health to reducing the risk of chronic diseases. Its emphasis on whole foods, lean proteins, and healthy fats provides balanced nutrition that supports overall well-being. This diet not only enhances physical health but also promotes a fulfilling lifestyle centered around good food and community.

Brain Health and Cognitive Function

The Mediterranean diet is rich in brain-boosting nutrients like omega-3 fatty acids, antioxidants, and vitamins that support cognitive function. Regular consumption of foods such as fish, nuts, and leafy greens can help protect against cognitive decline, improve memory, and promote long-term brain health.

Reducing Inflammation

Chronic inflammation is linked to many health issues, but the Mediterranean diet's focus on anti-inflammatory foods like olive oil, fatty fish, fruits, and vegetables can help reduce inflammation throughout the body. This dietary approach supports a healthier immune system and lowers the risk of conditions such as heart disease and arthritis.

Supporting Balanced Blood Sugar Levels

The Mediterranean diet's emphasis on whole grains, legumes, and fiber-rich vegetables helps maintain stable blood sugar levels. These foods are digested slowly, preventing blood sugar spikes and supporting better glucose control, making this diet beneficial for managing and preventing type 2 diabetes.

Weight Management

The Mediterranean diet naturally supports weight management by encouraging the consumption of nutrient-dense, satisfying foods. With a focus on fruits, vegetables, lean proteins, and healthy fats, this diet helps you feel full and energized without the need for strict calorie counting or deprivation.

Promoting Better Sleep

The Mediterranean diet promotes better sleep through balanced nutrition. The diet's emphasis on foods rich in magnesium, like leafy greens and nuts, along with healthy fats and lean proteins, helps regulate sleep cycles and improve sleep quality, leading to more restful nights.

The Advantages of Embracing Mediterranean Diet Cooking

Cooking with the Mediterranean diet is not only healthy but also enjoyable and accessible. Its focus on fresh, whole ingredients makes it easy to create meals that are both flavorful and nutritious. Whether you're a seasoned cook or just starting out, Mediterranean diet cooking offers a wide range of dishes that are simple to prepare and a pleasure to eat.

Budget-Friendly Ingredients

The Mediterranean diet relies on affordable, everyday ingredients like grains, legumes, seasonal vegetables, and olive oil. These staples are not only budget-friendly but also versatile, allowing you to create a variety of healthy meals without overspending.

Versatile Ingredients for Multiple Meals

The Mediterranean diet features versatile ingredients such as tomatoes, garlic, and olive oil that can be used across multiple dishes. This flexibility simplifies meal planning and ensures that you can create diverse and satisfying meals with minimal effort.

Investing in Quality Where It Matters

While the Mediterranean diet is affordable, it's important to invest in quality where it counts. Choosing high-quality olive oil, fresh produce, and sustainably sourced fish not only enhances flavor but also maximizes the nutritional benefits of your meals.

Cost-Saving Tips

Adopting the Mediterranean diet doesn't have to be expensive. Buying in-season produce, purchasing bulk staples like grains and beans, and minimizing waste through meal planning are effective ways to enjoy the diet's benefits while staying within your budget.

Exploring a Variety of Mediterranean Cuisines

The Mediterranean diet offers a rich variety of flavors and traditions from different cultures, including Greek, Italian, Middle Eastern, and North African cuisines. Exploring these diverse culinary traditions allows you to experience new tastes and keep your meals exciting and varied.

Minimal Equipment Required

The Mediterranean diet relies on affordable, Mediterranean cooking is accessible to everyone, requiring only basic kitchen tools like a good knife, cutting board, and a few pots and pans. With minimal equipment, you can prepare a wide range of delicious and healthy meals.

Simple Meal Planning

Meal planning is straightforward with the Mediterranean diet. Focus on fresh vegetables, whole grains, and lean proteins to build balanced meals that are easy to prepare and full of flavor. This simplicity makes it easy to maintain a healthy eating routine.

Quick and Nourishing Snack Ideas

The Mediterranean diet offers a variety of quick, healthy snack options such as fresh fruit, nuts, yogurt, and whole-grain crackers with hummus. These snacks are not only convenient but also provide sustained energy throughout the day, making them perfect for busy lifestyles.

Enjoy the Brand-New Diet and Lifestyle

Embark on a journey of flavor, health, and well-being with the Mediterranean diet—a brand-new approach to eating and living that blends time-honored traditions with modern convenience. This diet is not just about the food on your plate; it's a holistic lifestyle that nourishes your body, mind, and spirit. By embracing this way of eating, you're opening the door to a healthier, more balanced life filled with joy, vitality, and meals that are easy to prepare and a pleasure to share. Imagine savoring the sun-kissed flavors of ripe tomatoes, fresh herbs, and golden olive oil, all while making choices that benefit your long-term health. The Mediterranean diet invites you to slow down, enjoy the process of cooking, and reconnect with the simple pleasures of wholesome, real food. Whether you're cooking for yourself or entertaining friends, this lifestyle brings people together around the table, fostering connection, wellness, and long-lasting well-being. And the best part? You can indulge in delicious, nutrient-rich meals without sacrificing flavor or satisfaction. As you dive into this new way of living, you'll find it's more than just a diet—it's a joyful, sustainable approach to a healthier, happy life full of vitality.

Chapter ①

BREAKFAST and APPETIZERS

Greek Yogurt with Honey and Nuts

PREPARATION TIME: 5 MINUTES

COOKING TIME: NONE

SERVES: 4

Nutrition Information (Per Serving):
220 Calories / 9g Fat / 25g Carbohydrates / 12g Protein / 65 mg Sodium / 20g Sugar

INGREDIENTS:

- 2 cups Greek yogurt
- 4 tablespoons honey
- 1/2 cup of your favorite nuts, chopped (e.g., walnuts, almonds, pistachios)

DIRECTIONS:

1. Divide Greek yogurt evenly into 4 bowls.
2. Drizzle 1 tablespoon of honey over each bowl of yogurt.
3. Sprinkle your favorite chopped nuts on top of each serving.
4. Optionally, add a pinch of cinnamon or fresh berries for extra flavor
5. Serve immediately and enjoy!

TIP: Toast the nuts briefly in a skillet to enhance their flavor and add extra crunch to your yogurt.

Avocado Toast with Olive Oil

PREPARATION TIME: 5 MINUTES

COOKING TIME: 5 MINUTES

SERVES: 4

Nutrition Information (Per Serving):
250 Calories / 17g Fat / 22g Carbohydrates / 5g Protein / 150mg Sodium / 1g Sugar

INGREDIENTS:

- 2-3 ripe avocados
- 8 slices of whole-grain bread, or bread of your choice
- 4 tablespoons olive oil
- Salt and pepper to taste

DIRECTIONS:

1. Toast the bread until golden brown.
2. Mash the avocados in a bowl, leaving some chunks for texture.
3. Spread the mashed avocado on each slice of toast.
4. Drizzle one tablespoon of olive oil over each slice.
5. Season with salt and pepper.
6. Serve immediately.

TIP: Top with a poached egg or sliced tomatoes for added flavor.

Tomato and Feta Omelette

 PREPARATION TIME: 10 MINUTES

 COOKING TIME: 10 MINUTES

 SERVES: 4

Nutrition Information (Per Serving):
200 Calories / 14g Fat / 6g Carbohydrates / 12g Protein / 300mg Sodium / 3g Sugar

INGREDIENTS:

- 8 large eggs
- 1/2 cup crumbled feta cheese
- 1 cup cherry tomatoes, halved
- 2 tablespoons olive oil
- 1/4 cup chopped fresh basil (optional)
- Salt and pepper to taste

DIRECTIONS:

1. In a bowl, whisk the eggs until well combined. Season with salt and pepper.
2. Heat 1 tablespoon of olive oil in a non-stick pan over medium heat.
3. Pour in half of the egg mixture and cook for 2-3 minutes until the edges start to set.
4. Sprinkle half of the feta cheese and half of the cherry tomatoes over the eggs.
5. Cook for another 2-3 minutes until the eggs are fully set.
6. Fold the omelette in half and slide it onto a plate.
7. Repeat the process with the remaining egg mixture, feta, and tomatoes.
8. Garnish with fresh basil if desired, and serve immediately.

Simple Pita Bread with Hummus

 PREPARATION TIME: 5 MINUTES

 COOKING TIME: 5 MINUTES

 SERVES: 4

Nutrition Information (Per Serving):
240 Calories / 9g Fat / 30g Carbohydrates / 7g Protein / 360mg Sodium / 1g Sugar

INGREDIENTS:

- 4 whole pita breads
- 1 cup hummus (see recipe on p.22)
- 2 tablespoons olive oil
- Paprika for garnish
- Fresh parsley leaves (optional)

DIRECTIONS:

1. Cut each pita bread in half and place the halves in a toaster. Toast on a low setting for 1-2 minutes or until the bread is warm and slightly crisp
2. Spoon the hummus into a serving bowl.
3. Drizzle olive oil over the hummus.
4. Sprinkle paprika over the top.
5. Garnish with parsley leaves.
6. Dip pita in hummus and enjoy!

TIP: Serve the hummus with a side of sliced cucumber and cherry tomatoes for a refreshing, crunchy accompaniment

Mediterranean Smoothie

 PREPARATION TIME: 5 MINUTES

 COOKING TIME: NONE

SERVES: 4

Nutrition Information (Per Serving):
180 Calories / 6g Fat / 24g Carbohydrates / 8g Protein / 55mg Sodium / 18g Sugar

INGREDIENTS:

- 2 cups plain Greek yogurt
- 1 cup mixed berries (strawberries, blueberries, raspberries, blackberries)
- 1 medium banana
- 1/2 cup orange juice
- 1 tablespoon honey
- 1/4 teaspoon ground cinnamon
- Ice cubes (optional)

DIRECTIONS:

1. Combine the Greek yogurt, mixed berries, banana, orange juice, honey, and ground cinnamon in a blender.
2. Blend until smooth, adding ice cubes if a thicker texture is desired.
3. Pour the smoothie into four glasses and serve immediately.

TIP: Garnish each glass with a sprig of fresh mint for a refreshing finish

Bruschetta with Mozzarella, Tomato, and Pesto

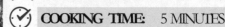 **PREPARATION TIME:** 10 MINUTES

 **COOKING TIME:** 5 MINUTES

SERVES: 4

Nutrition Information (Per Serving):
200 Calories / 12g Fat / 18g Carbohydrates / 8g Protein / 300mg Sodium / 2g Sugar

INGREDIENTS:

- 8 slices of crusty bread (like a baguette or ciabatta)
- 2 ripe tomatoes, diced
- 1 ball (about 8 oz) fresh mozzarella, sliced
- 1/4 cup pesto sauce (see recipe on p.23)
- 2 tablespoons olive oil
- Salt and pepper to taste
- Fresh basil leaves for garnish

DIRECTIONS:

1. Preheat a grill pan or oven broiler. Brush both sides of the bread slices with olive oil. Grill or broil the bread for 2-3 minutes on each side until golden and crispy.
2. Spread about 1 teaspoon of pesto on each slice of toasted bread. Top with a slice of fresh mozzarella and a spoonful of diced tomatoes.
3. Sprinkle the tomatoes with a pinch of salt and pepper. Garnish with fresh basil leaves. Serve immediately.

TIP: For extra flavor, drizzle the bruschetta with a balsamic glaze before serving.

Simple Shakshuka

PREPARATION TIME: 10 MINUTES

COOKING TIME: 20 MINUTES

SERVES: 4

Nutrition Information (Per Serving):
250 Calories / 14g Fat / 20g Carbohydrates / 10g Protein / 450mg Sodium / 6g Sugar

INGREDIENTS:

- 4 large eggs
- 1 can (14 oz) diced tomatoes
- 1 red bell pepper, diced
- 1 onion, chopped
- 2 garlic cloves, minced
- 2 tablespoons olive oil
- 1 teaspoon ground cumin
- 1 teaspoon paprika
- Salt and pepper to taste
- Fresh cilantro for garnish

DIRECTIONS:

1. Heat olive oil in a large skillet over medium heat. Add the chopped onion and diced bell pepper, and cook until softened, about 5 minutes.
2. Stir in the minced garlic, ground cumin, and paprika, and cook for another minute until fragrant.
3. Pour in the diced tomatoes and bring the mixture to a simmer. Season with salt and pepper to taste.
4. Make four small wells in the tomato mixture, and crack an egg into each well.
5. Cover the skillet and cook for 7-10 minutes, or until the eggs are set to your liking.
6. Garnish with fresh cilantro and serve immediately with crusty bread.

Quinoa Breakfast Bowl with Tomatoes

PREPARATION TIME: 10 MINUTES

COOKING TIME: 20 MINUTES

SERVES: 4

Nutrition Information (Per Serving):
230 Calories / 8g Fat / 30g Carbohydrates / 10g Protein / 300mg Sodium / 4g Sugar

INGREDIENTS:

- 1 cup quinoa
- 2 cups water
- 1 cup cherry tomatoes, halved
- 1/2 cup crumbled feta cheese
- 2 tablespoons olive oil
- Fresh basil for garnish
- Salt and pepper to taste

DIRECTIONS:

1. Rinse the quinoa under cold water. In a medium saucepan, bring the quinoa and water to a boil. Reduce heat, cover, and simmer for about 15 minutes, or until the water is absorbed and the quinoa is fluffy.
2. Divide the cooked quinoa into four bowls. Top each bowl with halved cherry tomatoes and crumbled feta cheese.
3. Drizzle with olive oil and season with salt and pepper.
4. Garnish with fresh basil leaves and serve warm.

TIP: Add a poached egg on top for extra protein and richness

Mediterranean Breakfast Skillet

 PREPARATION TIME: 10 MINUTES

 COOKING TIME: 20 MINUTES

 SERVES: 4

Nutrition Information (Per Serving):
300 Calories / 18g Fat / 20g Carbohydrates / 15g Protein / 450mg Sodium / 5g Sugar

INGREDIENTS:

- 4 large eggs
- 1 large potato, diced
- 1 bell pepper, diced
- 1/2 cup cherry tomatoes, halved
- 1/4 cup crumbled feta cheese
- 2 tablespoons olive oil
- 1 teaspoon smoked paprika
- Fresh parsley for garnish
- Salt and pepper to taste

DIRECTIONS:

1. Heat olive oil in a large skillet over medium heat. Add the diced potatoes and cook until they start to soften, about 10 minutes.
2. Add the diced bell pepper and cherry tomatoes, and cook for another 5 minutes until the vegetables are tender.
3. Sprinkle smoked paprika over the vegetables and stir to combine. Season with salt and pepper.
4. Make four small wells in the vegetable mixture, and crack an egg into each well.
5. Cover the skillet and cook until the eggs are set to your liking, about 5-7 minutes.
6. Sprinkle with crumbled feta and garnish with fresh parsley. Serve immediately.

Lemon Ricotta Pancakes

 PREPARATION TIME: 10 MINUTES

 COOKING TIME: 15 MINUTES

 SERVES: 4

Nutrition Information (Per Serving):
250 Calories / 14g Fat / 22g Carbohydrates / 9g Protein / 270mg Sodium / 4g Sugar

INGREDIENTS:

- 2 cups ricotta cheese
- 4 large eggs
- 1 cup whole milk
- 2 tablespoons lemon zest (from 2 lemons)
- 4 tablespoons fresh lemon juice
- 2 cups all-purpose flour
- 2 tablespoons sugar
- 2 teaspoons baking powder
- 1/2 teaspoon salt
- Olive oil or butter for cooking
- Fresh berries and honey, for serving (optional)

DIRECTIONS:

1. In a large bowl, whisk together the ricotta cheese, eggs, milk, lemon zest, and lemon juice until smooth.
2. In a separate bowl, mix the flour, sugar, baking powder, and salt.
3. Gradually add the dry ingredients to the ricotta mixture, stirring until just combined; the batter will be thick.
4. Heat a non-stick skillet over medium heat and add a small amount of olive oil or butter.
5. Pour about 1/4 cup of batter onto the skillet for each pancake. Cook until bubbles form on the surface, about 2-3 minutes. Flip and cook for another 2-3 minutes or until golden brown.
6. Serve warm, topped with fresh berries and a drizzle of honey.

Za'atar and Olive Oil Bread

 PREPARATION TIME: 10 MINUTES

 COOKING TIME: 15 MINUTES

SERVES: 4

Nutrition Information (Per Serving):
280 Calories / 14g Fat / 30g Carbohydrates / 6g Protein / 250mg Sodium / 2g Sugar

INGREDIENTS:

- 4 whole pita breads
- 1/4 cup olive oil
- 2 tablespoons za'atar spice blend
- Sea salt to taste

DIRECTIONS:

1. Preheat your oven to 350°F (175°C).
2. Place the pita breads on a baking sheet.
3. In a small bowl, mix the olive oil with the za'atar spice blend.
4. Brush the za'atar mixture evenly over the pita breads.
5. Sprinkle a pinch of sea salt on top.
6. Bake in the oven for 10-15 minutes, or until the bread is crispy and golden. Serve warm

TIP: Pair this bread with hummus or another sauce of your choice for dipping, or use it as a base for a simple Mediterranean-style pizza.

Mediterranean Fruit Bowl with Mint

 PREPARATION TIME: 10 MINUTES

 COOKING TIME: NONE

 SERVES: 4

Nutrition Information (Per Serving):
150 Calories / 2g Fat / 35g Carbohydrates / 2g Protein / 10mg Sodium / 30g Sugar

INGREDIENTS:

- 1 cup watermelon, cubed
- 1 cup cantaloupe, cubed
- 1 cup grapes, halved
- 1 cup fresh berries (strawberries, blueberries, or raspberries)
- 1 tablespoon fresh mint leaves, finely chopped
- Juice of 1 lemon or lime
- 1 tablespoon honey (optional)

DIRECTIONS:

1. In a large bowl, combine the watermelon, cantaloupe, grapes, and berries.
2. Drizzle the lemon or lime juice over the fruit, and add the chopped mint leaves.
3. If using, drizzle the honey over the fruit for added sweetness.
4. Gently toss the fruit mixture to combine, ensuring the fruit is evenly coated with the juice and mint.
5. Serve immediately or chill in the refrigerator for 15-20 minutes to allow the flavors to meld.

TIP: For a savory twist, sprinkle a little crumbled feta cheese over the fruit before serving, or add a few pomegranate seeds for extra color and flavor.

Çılbır (Turkish Poached Eggs with Yogurt)

 PREPARATION TIME: 10 MINUTES

 COOKING TIME: 10 MINUTES

 SERVES: 4

Nutrition Information (Per Serving):
250 Calories / 18g Fat / 6g Carbohydrates / 14g Protein / 150mg Sodium / 3g Sugar

INGREDIENTS:

- 4 large eggs
- 2 cups Greek yogurt
- 2 garlic cloves, minced
- 2 tablespoons butter
- 1 teaspoon paprika (or Aleppo pepper)
- 1 tablespoon olive oil
- 1 tablespoon white vinegar
- Fresh dill or parsley for garnish
- Salt and pepper to taste

DIRECTIONS:

1. Mix Greek yogurt with minced garlic and a pinch of salt. Divide the yogurt mixture among four plates.
2. Simmer water with vinegar in a medium saucepan. Crack each egg into a small bowl, then gently slide it into the simmering water. Poach the eggs for 3-4 minutes until the whites are set but the yolks remain runny. Remove the eggs with a slotted spoon and place one egg on each plate of yogurt.
3. In a small skillet, melt butter over medium heat. Once it begins to foam, add paprika and stir for about 30 seconds until fragrant. Remove from heat and stir in olive oil.
4. Drizzle the butter and paprika sauce over the poached eggs and yogurt. Garnish with fresh dill or parsley. Serve immediately with crusty bread.

Mediterranean Breakfast Wrap

 PREPARATION TIME: 10 MINUTES

 COOKING TIME: 15 MINUTES

 SERVES: 4

Nutrition Information (Per Serving):
280 Calories / 15g Fat / 25g Carbohydrates / 12g Protein / 500mg Sodium / 3g Sugar

INGREDIENTS:

- 4 large whole-wheat tortillas, or tortillas of your choice
- 1 cup hummus (see recipe on p.22)
- 1 cup fresh spinach leaves
- 1/2 cup diced tomatoes
- 1/2 cup crumbled feta cheese
- 1/4 cup sliced black olives (optional)
- Salt and pepper to taste

DIRECTIONS:

1. Lay the tortillas flat on a clean surface.
2. Evenly spread about 1/4 cup of hummus on each tortilla.
3. Layer fresh spinach leaves, diced tomatoes, and black olives (if using) on top of the hummus.
4. Sprinkle crumbled feta cheese over the vegetables.
5. Lightly season with salt and pepper.
6. Fold the sides of the tortilla inward, then roll it up tightly from the bottom to form a wrap.
7. Serve immediately or wrap in foil for an easy, portable breakfast.

Honey and Almond Oatmeal

 PREPARATION TIME: 5 MINUTES

 COOKING TIME: 10 MINUTES

SERVES: 4

Nutrition Information (Per Serving):
220 Calories / 8g Fat / 32g Carbohydrates / 6g Protein / 90mg Sodium / 10g Sugar

INGREDIENTS:

- 1 cup rolled oats
- 2 cups almond milk or milk of your choice
- 2 tablespoons honey
- 1/4 cup sliced almonds
- 1/2 teaspoon ground cinnamon

DIRECTIONS:

1. In a medium saucepan, bring the milk to a boil. Stir in the oats and cook for 5-7 minutes, until tender. Mix in the honey and cinnamon. Divide into bowls and top with sliced almonds before serving.
2. This recipe offers the flexibility to use your preferred type of milk, making it a versatile and delicious breakfast option.

TIP: For added texture and flavor, try stirring in a handful of fresh berries or a spoonful of nut butter before serving.

Bulgur Breakfast Bowl

 PREPARATION TIME: 10 MINUTES

 COOKING TIME: 15 MINUTES

SERVES: 4

Nutrition Information (Per Serving):
250 Calories / 10g Fat / 30g Carbohydrates / 8g Protein / 200mg Sodium / 4g Sugar

INGREDIENTS:

- 1 cup bulgur wheat
- 2 cups water
- 1 cup chopped cucumbers
- 1 cup chopped tomatoes
- 1/4 cup sliced in haft olives
- 2 tablespoons tahini sauce (see recipe on p.23)
- 2 tablespoons olive oil
- 4 soft-boiled eggs
- Fresh parsley for garnish
- Salt and pepper to taste

DIRECTIONS:

1. Cook the Bulgur: In a medium saucepan, bring the water to a boil. Add the bulgur wheat, reduce the heat to low, cover, and simmer for about 12-15 minutes, or until the water is absorbed and the bulgur is tender. Fluff with a fork.
2. Divide the cooked bulgur into four bowls. Top each bowl with chopped cucumbers, tomatoes, and sliced olives.
3. Drizzle tahini sauce and olive oil evenly over each bowl. Season with salt and pepper to taste.
4. Place a soft-boiled egg on top of each bowl. You can cut the egg in half to let the yolk run slightly.
5. Garnish with fresh parsley and serve immediately.

Mediterranean Breakfast Pizza

 PREPARATION TIME: 10 MINUTES

 COOKING TIME: 10 MINUTES

SERVES: 4

Nutrition Information (Per Serving):
320 Calories / 16g Fat / 30g Carbohydrates / 12g Protein / 400mg Sodium / 4g Sugar

INGREDIENTS:

- 4 whole-wheat pita breads
- 1/2 cup hummus (see recipe on p.22)
- 1/2 cup cherry tomatoes, halved
- 1/4 cup sliced black olives
- 1/4 cup crumbled feta cheese
- 4 large eggs
- 2 tablespoons olive oil
- Fresh basil or parsley for garnish
- Salt and pepper to taste

DIRECTIONS:

1. Preheat your oven to 375°F (190°C).
2. Place the pita breads on a baking sheet. Spread a layer of hummus evenly over each pita.
3. Top with cherry tomatoes, black olives, and crumbled feta cheese.
4. Drizzle a little olive oil over the toppings and season with salt and pepper.
5. Make a small well in the center of each pita and crack an egg into each well.
6. Bake in the preheated oven for 8-10 minutes, or until the egg whites are set and the yolks are cooked to your liking.
7. Garnish with fresh basil or parsley before serving.

Eggplant and Tomato Bake

 PREPARATION TIME: 15 MINUTES

COOKING TIME: 30 MINUTES

SERVES: 4

Nutrition Information (Per Serving):
200 Calories / 12g Fat / 18g Carbohydrates / 5g Protein / 220mg Sodium / 6g Sugar

INGREDIENTS:

- 1 large eggplant, sliced into rounds
- 3 large tomatoes, sliced
- 2 garlic cloves, minced
- 3 tablespoons olive oil
- 1/4 cup fresh basil leaves, chopped
- Salt and pepper to taste

DIRECTIONS:

1. Preheat your oven to 375°F (190°C).
2. Arrange the sliced eggplant and tomatoes in an alternating pattern in a large baking dish.
3. Sprinkle the minced garlic evenly over the eggplant and tomatoes. Drizzle with olive oil and season with salt and pepper.
4. Place the dish in the preheated oven and bake for about 25-30 minutes, or until the eggplant is tender and the tomatoes are slightly caramelized.
5. Once baked, sprinkle with fresh basil.

Spinach and Feta Scrambled Eggs

PREPARATION TIME: 5 MINUTES

COOKING TIME: 5 MINUTES

SERVES: 4

Nutrition Information (Per Serving):
180 Calories / 14g Fat / 3g Carbohydrates / 10g Protein / 250mg Sodium / 1g Sugar

INGREDIENTS:

- 8 large eggs
- 2 cups fresh spinach leaves
- 8 tablespoons crumbled feta cheese
- 2 tablespoon olive oil
- Salt and pepper to taste

DIRECTIONS:

1. In a bowl, beat the eggs with a pinch of salt and pepper.
2. Heat 1 tablespoon of olive oil in a pan over medium heat. Add the spinach and cook until wilted, about 2 minutes.
3. Pour the remaining olive oil into the pan. Add the beaten eggs to the spinach. Cook, stirring gently, until the eggs are just set.
4. Sprinkle the crumbled feta over the eggs and cook for an additional minute, allowing the cheese to warm and slightly melt.
5. Serve immediately, garnished with extra fresh herbs if desired.

TIP: For an extra burst of flavor, you can add a pinch of dried oregano or a squeeze of lemon juice just before serving.

Baked Zucchini Frittata

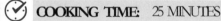

PREPARATION TIME: 10 MINUTES

COOKING TIME: 25 MINUTES

SERVES: 4

Nutrition Information (Per Serving):
180 Calories / 12g Fat / 7g Carbohydrates / 10g Protein / 250mg Sodium / 2g Sugar

INGREDIENTS:

- 4 large eggs
- 2 medium zucchinis, grated
- 1/2 cup grated Parmesan cheese
- 1/4 cup chopped fresh basil
- 2 tablespoons olive oil
- Salt and pepper to taste

DIRECTIONS:

1. Preheat your oven to 375°F (190°C).
2. In a large bowl, beat the eggs. Mix in the grated zucchini, Parmesan, basil, salt, and pepper.
3. Heat the olive oil in an ovenproof skillet over medium heat. Pour the egg mixture into the skillet and cook for 5 minutes until the edges start to set.
4. Transfer the skillet to the oven and bake for 20 minutes, or until the frittata is set and lightly golden.
5. Let cool slightly, slice into wedges, and serve warm or at room temperature.

TIP: Pair your frittata with a light drizzle of garlic aioli or a dollop of pesto for added flavor.

Mezze Platter

A mezze platter is a collection of small, flavorful dishes that are commonly enjoyed in Mediterranean and Middle Eastern cuisines. The term "mezze" refers to a variety of appetizers or small plates that are served together, creating a diverse and communal eating experience.

Mezze platters are often enjoyed as an appetizer before a main course but can also be served as a complete meal. The dishes on a mezze platter are designed to be shared, offering a range of tastes, textures, and aromas that complement each other.

A typical mezze platter may include items such as:

- **Greek Tzatziki Dip** (see recipe on p.21)
- **Hummus** (see recipe on p.22)
- **Baba Ghanoush** (see recipe on p.25)
- **Stuffed Grape Leaves (Dolmas)** (see recipe on p.43)
- **Pita bread, Crackers**
- **Assorted Fresh Vegetables**
- **Marinated Olives** (see recipe on p.46)
- **Feta Cheese**
- **Taramosalata (Greek Caviar Spread)** (see recipe on p.26)
- **Pickled Vegetables** (see recipe on p.48)
- **Various Salads of Your Choice**

The beauty of a mezze platter lies in its versatility—you can mix and match your favorite dishes to create a personalized and satisfying spread. Whether enjoyed with family, friends, or guests, a mezze platter is a wonderful way to experience the rich and diverse flavors of the Mediterranean and Middle Eastern regions.

Chapter ②

SAUCES and DIPS

Greek Tzatziki Dip

PREPARATION TIME: 10 MINUTES

COOKING TIME: NONE

CHILLING TIME: 30 MINUTES

SERVES: 4

Nutrition Information (Per Serving):
100 Calories / 6g Fat / 6g Carbohydrates / 4g Protein / 60mg Sodium / 4g Sugar

INGREDIENTS:

- 1 cup Greek yogurt
- 1 cucumber, grated and drained
- 2 garlic cloves, minced
- 1 tablespoon olive oil
- 1 tablespoon fresh lemon juice
- 1 tablespoon chopped fresh dill
- Salt and pepper to taste

DIRECTIONS:

1. Grate the cucumber and squeeze out the excess water using a clean kitchen towel or paper towels.
2. In a medium bowl, combine the Greek yogurt, grated cucumber, minced garlic, olive oil, and lemon juice.
3. Stir in the chopped dill and season with salt and pepper.
4. Mix well until all ingredients are fully combined.
5. Refrigerate for at least 30 minutes to allow the flavors to meld.
6. Serve chilled with pita bread, fresh vegetables, or as a sauce for grilled meats.

Hummus with Olive Oil and Paprika

PREPARATION TIME: 10 MINUTES

COOKING TIME: 5 MINUTES

SERVES: 4

Nutrition Information (Per Serving):
180 Calories / 12g Fat / 14g Carbohydrates / 6g Protein / 240mg Sodium / 1g Sugar

INGREDIENTS:

- 1 can (15 oz) chickpeas, drained and rinsed
- 1/4 cup tahini sauce (see recipe on p.22)
- 2 tablespoons lemon juice
- 1 garlic clove, minced
- 2 tablespoons extra virgin olive oil, plus more for drizzling
- 1/2 teaspoon ground cumin
- Salt to taste
- Water, as needed for consistency
- 1/2 teaspoon paprika, for garnish

DIRECTIONS:

1. In a food processor, combine the chickpeas, tahini, lemon juice, garlic, olive oil, cumin, and salt.
2. Blend until smooth, adding water a tablespoon at a time until desired consistency is reached.
3. Transfer the hummus to a serving bowl and drizzle with olive oil.
4. Sprinkle with paprika for garnish.
5. Serve with pita bread, vegetables, or as desired.

Simple Pesto

 PREPARATION TIME: 10 MINUTES

 COOKING TIME: NONE

 SERVES: 4

Nutrition Information (Per Serving):
200 Calories / 20g Fat / 2g Carbohydrates / 3g Protein / 150mg Sodium / 0g Sugar

INGREDIENTS:

- 2 cups fresh basil leaves
- 1/2 cup extra virgin olive oil
- 1/3 cup pine nuts or walnuts
- 2 cloves garlic, minced
- 1/2 cup grated Parmesan cheese
- Salt and pepper to taste
- Optional: a squeeze of lemon juice

DIRECTIONS:

1. In a food processor, combine the basil leaves, nuts, and garlic. Pulse until finely chopped.
2. While the processor is running, slowly drizzle in the olive oil until the mixture is smooth.
3. Add the grated Parmesan cheese, and pulse until combined.
4. Season with salt, pepper, and optionally, a squeeze of lemon juice to brighten the flavor.
5. Serve immediately or store in an airtight container in the refrigerator.

Tahini Sauce

 PREPARATION TIME: 10 MINUTES

 COOKING TIME: NONE

SERVES: 4

Nutrition Information (Per Serving):
160 Calories / 14g Fat / 5g Carbohydrates / 4g Protein / 100mg Sodium / 0g Sugar

INGREDIENTS:

- 1/2 cup crushed sesame seeds
- 1/4 cup water (adjust for desired consistency)
- 2 tablespoons lemon juice
- 1 garlic clove, minced
- Salt to taste
- Optional: a pinch of ground cumin or paprika

DIRECTIONS:

1. In a bowl, whisk together the crushed sesame seeds and lemon juice until well combined.
2. Gradually add water, whisking until the sauce reaches your desired consistency.
3. Stir in the minced garlic and salt to taste.
4. Optionally, add a pinch of cumin or paprika for extra flavor.
5. Serve immediately or refrigerate in an airtight container.

Skordalia (Garlic-Potato Dip)

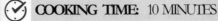
PREPARATION TIME: 15 MINUTES

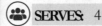
COOKING TIME: 10 MINUTES

SERVES: 4

Nutrition Information (Per Serving):
180 Calories / 12g Fat / 15g Carbohydrates / 3g Protein / 200mg Sodium / 2g Sugar

INGREDIENTS:

- 4 medium potatoes, peeled and chopped
- 4 cloves garlic, minced
- 1/4 cup extra virgin olive oil
- 2 tablespoons lemon juice
- 1/4 cup warm water
- Salt and pepper to taste
- Optional: 2 tablespoons white wine vinegar

DIRECTIONS:

1. Boil the chopped potatoes in salted water for about 10 minutes, or until tender. Drain and set aside.
2. In a food processor, combine the garlic, olive oil, lemon juice, and warm water.
3. Add the boiled potatoes to the processor and blend until smooth and creamy.
4. Season with salt and pepper to taste.
5. Optionally, add white wine vinegar for a tangier flavor.
6. Serve as a dip with bread, vegetables, or as a sauce for grilled meats.

TIP: For extra flavor, add a handful of chopped fresh herbs like parsley or dill to the dip.

Roasted Red Pepper Dip

PREPARATION TIME: 10 MINUTES

COOKING TIME: 5 MINUTES (if roasting peppers yourself)

SERVES: 4

Nutrition Information (Per Serving):
150 Calories / 10g Fat / 13g Carbohydrates / 3g Protein / 200mg Sodium / 4g Sugar

INGREDIENTS:

- 2 large roasted red peppers (jarred or homemade)
- 1/4 cup tahini sauce (see recipe on p.21)
- 2 tablespoons lemon juice
- 1 garlic clove, minced
- 2 tablespoons extra virgin olive oil
- 1/2 teaspoon ground cumin
- Salt and pepper to taste
- 1/4 teaspoon smoked paprika (optional)
- Fresh parsley for garnish (optional)

DIRECTIONS:

1. If using fresh red peppers, roast them over an open flame or under a broiler until the skin is charred. Let cool, then peel and remove seeds.
2. In a food processor, combine the roasted red peppers, tahini, lemon juice, garlic, olive oil, cumin, salt, and pepper.
3. Blend until smooth, adjusting seasoning to taste.
4. Transfer the dip to a serving bowl and drizzle with olive oil.
5. Optionally, sprinkle with smoked paprika and garnish with fresh parsley.
6. Serve with pita bread, crackers, or fresh vegetables.

Baba Ganoush

 PREPARATION TIME: 10 MINUTES

 COOKING TIME: 30 MINUTES

SERVES: 4

Nutrition Information (Per Serving):
120 Calories / 10g Fat / 8g Carbohydrates / 2g Protein / 150mg Sodium / 3g Sugar

INGREDIENTS:

- 2 large eggplants
- 1/4 cup tahini sauce (see recipe on p.22)
- 2 tablespoons lemon juice
- 2 cloves garlic, minced
- 2 tablespoons extra virgin olive oil, plus more for drizzling
- Salt and pepper to taste
- Optional: 1/4 teaspoon ground cumin
- Fresh parsley for garnish

DIRECTIONS:

1. Preheat your oven to 400°F (200°C).
2. Pierce the eggplants with a fork and place them on a baking sheet. Roast in the oven for about 30 minutes, turning occasionally, until the skin is charred and the flesh is soft.
3. Once roasted, let the eggplants cool slightly, then peel off the skin and discard it. Place the flesh in a colander to drain any excess liquid.
4. In a food processor, combine the roasted eggplant flesh, tahini, lemon juice, garlic, olive oil, salt, and pepper. Add ground cumin if desired.
5. Blend until smooth and creamy, adjusting seasoning to taste.
6. Transfer the Baba Ganoush to a serving bowl, drizzle with a little olive oil, and garnish with fresh parsley.
7. Serve with pita bread, crackers, or fresh vegetables.

Aioli (Mediterranean Garlic Mayonnaise)

 PREPARATION TIME: 10 MINUTES

 COOKING TIME: NONE

 SERVES: 4

Nutrition Information (Per Serving):
180 Calories / 18g Fat / 1g Carbohydrates / 1g Protein / 120mg Sodium / 0g Sugar

INGREDIENTS:

- 4 cloves garlic, minced
- 1 large egg yolk, at room temperature
- 1 cup extra virgin olive oil
- 1 tablespoon lemon juice
- 1 teaspoon Dijon mustard (optional, for stability)
- Salt to taste
- Optional: a pinch of ground black pepper or paprika

DIRECTIONS:

1. In a medium bowl, whisk together the minced garlic, egg yolk, and Dijon mustard (if using) until well combined.
2. Begin adding the olive oil very slowly, almost drop by drop, while continuously whisking. This allows the oil to emulsify with the egg yolk, creating a thick, creamy sauce.
3. As the mixture thickens, you can gradually increase the speed at which you add the olive oil, but continue whisking vigorously to maintain the emulsion.
4. Once all the oil is incorporated, stir in the lemon juice and season with salt. Add a pinch of ground black pepper or paprika if desired.
5. Taste and adjust the seasoning if necessary.
6. Transfer the aioli to a serving dish and serve immediately or refrigerate until ready to use.

Taramosalata (Greek Caviar Spread)

PREPARATION TIME: 15 MINUTES

COOKING TIME: NONE

SERVES: 4

Nutrition Information (Per Serving):
190 Calories / 14g Fat / 12g Carbohydrates / 4g Protein / 300mg Sodium / 1g Sugar

INGREDIENTS:

- 1/2 cup tarama (fish roe, typically from carp or cod)
- 2 slices of stale white bread, crusts removed
- 1 small onion, grated or finely chopped
- 1/2 cup olive oil
- 2 tablespoons lemon juice
- 1-2 tablespoons water (optional, for adjusting consistency)
- Salt and pepper to taste

DIRECTIONS:

1. Soak the bread slices in water for a few minutes, then squeeze out the excess water.
2. In a food processor, combine the tarama (fish roe), soaked bread, grated onion, and lemon juice. Blend until smooth.
3. Slowly add the olive oil in a steady stream while the food processor is running, allowing the mixture to emulsify and become creamy.
4. If the mixture is too thick, you can add 1-2 tablespoons of water to adjust the consistency.
5. Season with salt and pepper to taste, blending again to incorporate.
6. Transfer the taramosalata to a serving bowl and garnish with a drizzle of olive oil and a sprinkle of fresh herbs, if desired.
7. Serve with pita bread, fresh vegetables, or as part of a mezze platter.

Homemade Hot Honey

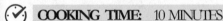

PREPARATION TIME: 5 MINUTES

COOKING TIME: 10 MINUTES

SERVES: 1 Cup   (approximately 16 tablespoons)

Nutrition Information (Per Tablespoon):
60 Calories / 0g Fat / 17g Carbohydrates / 0g Protein / 0mg Sodium / 17g Sugar

INGREDIENTS:

- 1 cup honey
- 1-2 tablespoons crushed red pepper flakes (adjust to taste)
- 1 teaspoon apple cider vinegar (optional, for a tangy kick)

DIRECTIONS:

1. In a small saucepan, combine the honey and crushed red pepper flakes.
2. Heat over low heat, stirring occasionally, for about 10 minutes. Do not let the honey boil; you want to gently warm it to extract the heat from the pepper flakes.
3. If you like a bit of tanginess, stir in the apple cider vinegar after removing the honey from the heat (add vinegar (Optional))
4. Allow the honey to cool slightly, then strain it through a fine-mesh sieve to remove the pepper flakes (optional, if you prefer a smoother texture).
5. Transfer the hot honey to a clean jar and store it at room temperature.

TIP: Drizzle over pizza, fried chicken, roasted vegetables, or use it in salad dressings.

Chapter ③

SALADS and SOUPS

Greek Salad

 PREPARATION TIME: 10 MINUTES

 COOKING TIME: NONE

SERVES: 4

Nutrition Information (Per Serving):
150 Calories / 12g Fat / 9g Carbohydrates / 3g Protein / 500mg Sodium / 4g Sugar

INGREDIENTS:

- 4 medium tomatoes, chopped
- 1 cucumber, sliced
- 1 red onion, thinly sliced
- 1 green bell pepper, sliced
- 1/2 cup Kalamata olives
- 7 oz feta cheese, cut into cubes or crumbled
- 1/4 cup extra virgin olive oil
- 1 tablespoon red wine vinegar
- 1 teaspoon dried oregano
- Salt and pepper to taste

DIRECTIONS:

1. In a large bowl, combine the chopped tomatoes, cucumber slices, red onion slices, green bell pepper slices, and Kalamata olives.
2. Add the cubed or crumbled feta cheese on top of the vegetables.
3. Drizzle the olive oil and red wine vinegar over the salad.
4. Sprinkle with dried oregano, salt, and pepper to taste.
5. Toss the salad gently to combine all the ingredients, ensuring the feta stays somewhat intact.
6. Serve immediately or chill for a few minutes before serving for a more refreshing experience.

Mediterranean Chickpea Salad

 PREPARATION TIME: 15 MINUTES

 COOKING TIME: NONE

 SERVES: 4

Nutrition Information (Per Serving):
220 Calories / 10g Fat / 25g Carbohydrates / 7g Protein / 400mg Sodium / 4g Sugar

INGREDIENTS:

- 1 can (15 oz) chickpeas, drained and rinsed
- 1 cucumber, diced
- 1 red bell pepper, diced
- 1/2 red onion, finely chopped
- 1/2 cup cherry tomatoes, halved
- 1/4 cup Kalamata olives, sliced
- 1/4 cup feta cheese, crumbled
- 2 tablespoons chopped fresh parsley
- 2 tablespoons extra virgin olive oil
- 1 tablespoon red wine vinegar or lemon juice
- 1 teaspoon dried oregano
- Salt and pepper to taste

DIRECTIONS:

1. In a large bowl, combine the chickpeas, diced cucumber, red bell pepper, red onion, cherry tomatoes, and Kalamata olives.
2. Add the crumbled feta cheese and chopped fresh parsley to the mixture.
3. In a small bowl, whisk together the olive oil, red wine vinegar or lemon juice, dried oregano, salt, and pepper.
4. Pour the dressing over the salad ingredients and toss gently to combine.
5. Taste and adjust seasoning if necessary.
6. Serve immediately or chill in the refrigerator for a more refreshing taste.

Cucumber Feta Salad

 PREPARATION TIME: 10 MINUTES

 COOKING TIME: NONE

SERVES: 4

Nutrition Information (Per Serving):
120 Calories / 9g Fat / 7g Carbohydrates / 3g Protein /
350mg Sodium / 3g Sugar

INGREDIENTS:

- 2 large cucumbers, peeled (if preferred) and sliced
- 1/2 cup feta cheese, crumbled
- 1/4 red onion, thinly sliced
- 2 tablespoons extra virgin olive oil
- 1 tablespoon red wine vinegar or lemon juice
- 1 tablespoon chopped fresh dill or mint (optional)
- Salt and pepper to taste

DIRECTIONS:

1. In a large bowl, combine the sliced cucumbers and red onion.
2. Add the crumbled feta cheese to the bowl.
3. Drizzle the olive oil and red wine vinegar or lemon juice over the salad.
4. Add the chopped fresh dill or mint, if using, and season with salt and pepper.
5. Toss gently to combine all ingredients.
6. Serve immediately or chill in the refrigerator for a more refreshing taste.

Arugula and Parmesan Salad

 PREPARATION TIME: 5 MINUTES

 COOKING TIME: NONE

 SERVES: 4

Nutrition Information (Per Serving):
110 Calories / 9g Fat / 4g Carbohydrates / 4g Protein /
220mg Sodium / 1g Sugar

INGREDIENTS:

- 4 cups fresh arugula leaves
- 1/4 cup shaved Parmesan cheese
- 2 tablespoons extra virgin olive oil
- 1 tablespoon lemon juice
- Salt and pepper to taste
- Optional: 1/4 cup toasted pine nuts or walnuts

DIRECTIONS:

1. Place the arugula leaves in a large salad bowl.
2. Drizzle the olive oil and lemon juice over the arugula.
3. Toss the salad gently to coat the arugula evenly with the dressing.
4. Sprinkle the shaved Parmesan cheese over the salad.
5. Season with salt and pepper to taste.
6. Optionally, add toasted pine nuts or walnuts for extra texture and flavor.
7. Serve immediately as a light and refreshing side dish.

Simple Olive Tapenade Salad

 PREPARATION TIME: 10 MINUTES

 COOKING TIME: NONE

 SERVES: 4

Nutrition Information (Per Serving):
250 Calories / 8g Fat / 35g Carbohydrates / 12g Protein / 450mg Sodium / 5g Sugar

INGREDIENTS:

- 1 cup mixed olives (Kalamata, green, etc.), pitted and chopped
- 1 tablespoon capers, rinsed and chopped
- 1 garlic clove, minced
- 2 tablespoons extra virgin olive oil
- 1 tablespoon lemon juice
- 1 teaspoon chopped fresh thyme or rosemary
- 4 cups mixed salad greens (arugula, spinach, etc.)
- Salt and pepper to taste

DIRECTIONS:

1. In a small bowl, combine the chopped olives, capers, minced garlic, olive oil, lemon juice, and fresh thyme or rosemary. Mix well to create the olive tapenade.
2. Place the mixed salad greens in a large salad bowl.
3. Spoon the olive tapenade over the greens.
4. Toss the salad gently to distribute the tapenade evenly.
5. Season with salt and pepper to taste.
6. Add a few whole olives on top.
7. Serve immediately as a flavorful and savory salad.

Lentil Soup

 PREPARATION TIME: 10 MINUTES

 COOKING TIME: 30-40 MINUTES

 SERVES: 4

Nutrition Information (Per Serving):
110 Calories / 9g Fat / 4g Carbohydrates / 4g Protein / 220mg Sodium / 1g Sugar

INGREDIENTS:

- 1 cup dried lentils, rinsed and drained
- 1 onion, chopped
- 2 carrots, diced
- 2 celery stalks, diced
- 3 garlic cloves, minced
- 2 tablespoons olive oil
- 1 teaspoon ground cumin
- 1 teaspoon ground coriander
- 1/2 teaspoon smoked paprika (optional)
- 1 bay leaf
- 6 cups vegetable broth or water
- 1 can (14.5 oz) diced tomatoes
- Salt and pepper to taste
- 2 tablespoons chopped fresh parsley or cilantro (optional, for garnish)
- Lemon wedges (optional, for serving)

DIRECTIONS:

1. In a large pot, heat the olive oil over medium heat.
2. Add the chopped onion, carrots, and celery. Cook for 5-7 minutes until the vegetables are softened.
3. Stir in the minced garlic, ground cumin, ground coriander, and smoked paprika (if using). Cook for another 1-2 minutes until fragrant.
4. Add the rinsed lentils, bay leaf, and vegetable broth or water to the pot. Bring to a boil.
5. Reduce the heat to low and simmer for 20-30 minutes, or until the lentils are tender.
6. Stir in the diced tomatoes and cook for an additional 5-10 minutes.
7. Remove the bay leaf and season the soup with salt and pepper to taste.
8. Serve the soup hot, garnished with chopped fresh parsley or cilantro if desired, and with lemon wedges on the side.

Tomato Basil Soup

 PREPARATION TIME: 10 MINUTES

 COOKING TIME: 25 MINUTES

 SERVES: 4

Nutrition Information (Per Serving):
180 Calories / 9g Fat / 22g Carbohydrates / 4g Protein / 400mg Sodium / 8g Sugar

INGREDIENTS:

- 2 tablespoons olive oil
- 1 onion, chopped
- 3 cloves garlic, minced
- 1 can (28 oz) crushed tomatoes
- 2 cups vegetable broth or water
- 1/2 cup fresh basil leaves, chopped
- 1 teaspoon sugar (optional, to balance acidity)
- Salt and pepper to taste
- 1/4 cup heavy cream or half-and-half (optional, for creamier texture)
- Fresh basil leaves for garnish

DIRECTIONS:

1. In a large pot, heat the olive oil over medium heat.
2. Add the chopped onion and cook for 5-7 minutes until softened.
3. Stir in the minced garlic and cook for another 1-2 minutes until fragrant.
4. Add the crushed tomatoes and vegetable broth or water to the pot. Stir to combine.
5. Bring the soup to a simmer and cook for 15-20 minutes to allow the flavors to meld.
6. Stir in the chopped fresh basil and sugar (if using). Season with salt and pepper to taste.
7. For a creamier texture, stir in the heavy cream or half-and-half just before serving.
8. Use an immersion blender to puree the soup until smooth, or leave it slightly chunky if preferred.
9. Serve the soup hot, garnished with fresh basil leaves.

Avgolemono (Greek Lemon Chicken Soup)

 PREPARATION TIME: 10 MINUTES

 COOKING TIME: 30 MINUTES

 SERVES: 4

Nutrition Information (Per Serving):
250 Calories / 10g Fat / 18g Carbohydrates / 20g Protein / 500mg Sodium / 2g Sugar

INGREDIENTS:

- 4 cups chicken broth
- 1/2 cup orzo pasta or rice
- 2 cups cooked chicken, shredded
- 2 large eggs
- 1/4 cup fresh lemon juice (about 2 lemons)
- Salt and pepper to taste
- 2 tablespoons chopped fresh parsley or dill (optional, for garnish)
- Lemon wedges for serving

DIRECTIONS:

1. In a large pot, bring the chicken broth to a boil over medium-high heat.
2. Add the orzo or rice to the broth and cook according to package instructions until tender, about 8-10 minutes.
3. Reduce the heat to low and stir in the shredded chicken. Allow it to heat through while preparing the egg-lemon mixture.
4. In a medium bowl, whisk together the eggs and fresh lemon juice until well combined.
5. Slowly ladle about 1 cup of the hot broth into the egg-lemon mixture, whisking constantly to temper the eggs and prevent curdling.
6. Gradually pour the tempered egg mixture back into the soup, stirring continuously until the soup thickens slightly, about 2-3 minutes. Do not let the soup boil.
7. Season the soup with salt and pepper to taste.
8. Serve the soup hot, garnished with chopped fresh parsley or dill if desired, and with lemon wedges on the side for an extra burst of lemon flavor.

Roasted Red Pepper Soup

 PREPARATION TIME: 10 MINUTES

 COOKING TIME: 30 MINUTES

 SERVES: 4

Nutrition Information (Per Serving):
180 Calories / 10g Fat / 18g Carbohydrates / 4g Protein / 350mg Sodium / 7g Sugar

INGREDIENTS:

- 5-6 large red bell peppers
- 2 tablespoons olive oil
- 1 onion, chopped
- 3 cloves garlic, minced
- 4 cups vegetable broth
- 1 teaspoon smoked paprika (optional)
- 1/4 teaspoon cayenne pepper (optional, for heat)
- Salt and pepper to taste
- 1/2 cup heavy cream or coconut milk (optional, for creaminess)
- Fresh basil or parsley for garnish

DIRECTIONS:

1. Preheat oven to 400°F (200°C). Roast red bell peppers on a baking sheet for 20-25 minutes, turning occasionally, until charred. Place in a bowl, cover with plastic wrap, and let steam for 10 minutes. Peel, seed, and roughly chop.
2. In a large pot, heat olive oil over medium heat. Sauté onion for 5-7 minutes until softened. Add garlic and cook for 1-2 minutes until fragrant.
3. Add chopped roasted peppers and broth to the pot. Stir in smoked paprika and cayenne, if using. Simmer for 10-15 minutes.
4. Puree the soup with an immersion blender or in batches in a regular blender. Return to the pot.
5. Stir in heavy cream or coconut milk, if desired. Season with salt and pepper. Serve hot, garnished with basil or parsley.

White Bean Soup

 PREPARATION TIME: 10 MINUTES

 COOKING TIME: 30 MINUTES

 SERVES: 4

Nutrition Information (Per Serving):
220 Calories / 8g Fat / 30g Carbohydrates / 10g Protein / 500mg Sodium / 2g Sugar

INGREDIENTS:

- 2 tablespoons olive oil
- 1 onion, chopped
- 2 cloves garlic, minced
- 2 carrots, diced
- 2 celery stalks, diced
- 4 cups vegetable or chicken broth
- 2 cans (15 oz each) white beans, drained and rinsed
- 1 can (14.5 oz) diced tomatoes
- 1 teaspoon dried thyme
- 1 bay leaf
- Salt and pepper to taste
- 2 cups spinach or kale, chopped (optional)
- Fresh parsley for garnish

DIRECTIONS:

1. In a large pot, heat olive oil over medium heat. Sauté onion, carrots, and celery for 5-7 minutes until softened.
2. Add garlic and cook for another 1-2 minutes until fragrant.
3. Stir in the broth, white beans, diced tomatoes, thyme, and bay leaf. Bring to a boil, then reduce heat and simmer for 20 minutes.
4. If using, add spinach or kale and cook for another 5 minutes until wilted.
5. Remove the bay leaf. Season with salt and pepper to taste.
6. Serve hot, garnished with fresh parsley.

Watermelon and Feta Salad

 PREPARATION TIME: 10 MINUTES

 COOKING TIME: NONE

 SERVES: 4

Nutrition Information (Per Serving):
150 Calories / 8g Fat / 18g Carbohydrates / 4g Protein / 250mg Sodium / 14g Sugar

INGREDIENTS:

- 4 cups watermelon, cubed
- 1 cup feta cheese, crumbled
- 1/4 cup fresh mint leaves, chopped
- 2 tablespoons olive oil
- 1 tablespoon balsamic glaze or balsamic vinegar
- Salt and pepper to taste

DIRECTIONS:

1. In a large bowl, combine the watermelon cubes, crumbled feta, and chopped mint.
2. Drizzle with olive oil and balsamic glaze or vinegar.
3. Toss gently to combine.
4. Season with salt and pepper to taste.
5. Serve immediately and enjoy a refreshing and flavorful salad.

Lebanese Tabbouleh Salad

 PREPARATION TIME: 15 MINUTES

 COOKING TIME: NONE

 SERVES: 4

Nutrition Information (Per Serving):
120 Calories / 7g Fat / 13g Carbohydrates / 2g Protein / 150mg Sodium / 2g Sugar

INGREDIENTS:

- 1/2 cup bulgur wheat
- 1 cup boiling water
- 2 cups fresh parsley, finely chopped
- 1/2 cup fresh mint, finely chopped
- 2 tomatoes, diced
- 1 cucumber, diced
- 4 green onions, finely chopped
- 1/4 cup fresh lemon juice
- 1/4 cup extra virgin olive oil
- Salt and pepper to taste

DIRECTIONS:

1. Place the bulgur wheat in a large bowl and pour the boiling water over it. Cover and let it soak for about 15 minutes, or until tender. Drain any excess water.
2. In a separate large bowl, combine the chopped parsley, mint, tomatoes, cucumber, and green onions.
3. Add the soaked bulgur wheat to the bowl with the vegetables.
4. Drizzle the lemon juice and olive oil over the mixture.
5. Season with salt and pepper to taste.
6. Toss gently to combine all the ingredients.
7. Serve chilled or at room temperature as a refreshing side dish.

Piyaz (Turkish White Bean Salad)

PREPARATION TIME: 15 MINUTES

COOKING TIME: NONE

SERVES: 4

Nutrition Information (Per Serving):
200 Calories / 10g Fat / 20g Carbohydrates / 6g Protein / 400mg Sodium / 3g Sugar

INGREDIENTS:

- 2 cans (15 oz) white beans, drained
- 1 small red onion, thinly sliced
- 1/2 cup chopped fresh parsley
- 1/2 cup halved cherry tomatoes
- 1/4 cup olive oil
- 2 tbsp red wine vinegar or lemon juice
- 1 tsp sumac (optional)
- Salt and pepper to taste
- 2 hard-boiled eggs, quartered (optional)
- Olives (optional)

DIRECTIONS:

1. In a large bowl, combine the white beans, sliced red onion, chopped parsley, and cherry tomatoes.
2. In a small bowl, whisk together the olive oil, red wine vinegar or lemon juice, sumac (if using), salt, and pepper.
3. Pour the dressing over the bean mixture and toss gently to combine.
4. Taste and adjust seasoning if needed.
5. Garnish with hard-boiled eggs and olives, if desired.
6. Serve immediately or chill for a few minutes before serving.

Caldo Verde (Portuguese Kale and Sausage Soup)

PREPARATION TIME: 15 MINUTES

COOKING TIME: 30 MINUTES

SERVES: 4

Nutrition Information (Per Serving):
250 Calories / 15g Fat / 20g Carbohydrates / 10g Protein / 700mg Sodium / 2g Sugar

INGREDIENTS:

- 2 tablespoons olive oil
- 1 onion, finely chopped
- 2 cloves garlic, minced
- 4 medium potatoes, peeled and thinly sliced
- 6 cups chicken or vegetable broth
- 1/2 pound Portuguese chorizo or smoked sausage, sliced
- 4 cups kale, stems removed and leaves thinly sliced
- Salt and pepper to taste
- Lemon wedges for serving (optional)

DIRECTIONS:

1. In a large pot, heat the olive oil over medium heat. Add the chopped onion and sauté for about 5 minutes, until softened. Add the minced garlic and cook for another 1-2 minutes, until fragrant.
2. Add the sliced potatoes to the pot and pour in the broth. Bring to a boil, then reduce the heat and simmer for about 15 minutes, until the potatoes are tender.
3. Use an immersion blender to puree the soup until smooth, or leave some chunks of potato for texture, if preferred.
4. Stir in the sliced sausage and cook for another 5 minutes to allow the flavors to meld. Add the thinly sliced kale and simmer for an additional 5 minutes, until the kale is wilted but still vibrant green.
5. Season with salt and pepper to taste. Serve the soup hot, with lemon wedges on the side if desired.

Simple Orzo Pasta Salad

 PREPARATION TIME: 10 MINUTES

 COOKING TIME: 10 MINUTES

 SERVES: 4

Nutrition Information (Per Serving):
220 Calories / 8g Fat / 30g Carbohydrates / 6g Protein / 350mg Sodium / 2g Sugar

INGREDIENTS:

- 1 cup orzo pasta
- 1/2 cup cherry tomatoes, halved
- 1/2 cucumber, diced
- 1/4 cup red onion, finely chopped
- 1/4 cup Kalamata olives, sliced
- 1/4 cup feta cheese, crumbled
- 2 tablespoons fresh parsley, chopped
- 2 tablespoons olive oil
- 1 tablespoon lemon juice
- Salt and pepper to taste

DIRECTIONS:

1. Bring a large pot of salted water to a boil. Add the orzo and cook according to package instructions, about 8-10 minutes. Drain and rinse under cold water to cool.
2. In a large bowl, combine the halved cherry tomatoes, diced cucumber, chopped red onion, sliced Kalamata olives, and crumbled feta cheese.
3. Add the cooked orzo to the bowl with the vegetables. Drizzle with olive oil and lemon juice.
4. Season with salt and pepper to taste. Toss gently to combine all the ingredients.
5. Serve the salad chilled or at room temperature, garnished with chopped fresh parsley.

Caprese Salad

 PREPARATION TIME: 10 MINUTES

 COOKING TIME: NONE

 SERVES: 4

Nutrition Information (Per Serving):
200 Calories / 16g Fat / 6g Carbohydrates / 7g Protein / 150mg Sodium / 4g Sugar

INGREDIENTS:

- 3-4 large ripe tomatoes, sliced
- 1 pound fresh mozzarella cheese, sliced
- 1/4 cup fresh basil leaves
- 2 tablespoons extra virgin olive oil
- 1 tablespoon balsamic glaze (optional)
- Salt and pepper to taste

DIRECTIONS:

1. Arrange the tomato slices and mozzarella slices alternately on a large platter, slightly overlapping them.
2. Tuck fresh basil leaves between the tomato and mozzarella slices.
3. Drizzle the salad with extra virgin olive oil, and balsamic glaze if using.
4. Season with salt and pepper to taste.
5. Serve the salad immediately, as a refreshing and elegant side dish.

Mediterranean Tuna Salad

 PREPARATION TIME: 10 MINUTES

 COOKING TIME: NONE

 SERVES: 4

Nutrition Information (Per Serving):
250 Calories / 15g Fat / 10g Carbohydrates / 22g Protein / 400mg Sodium / 2g Sugar

INGREDIENTS:

- 2 cans (5 oz each) tuna in olive oil, drained
- 1 cup cherry tomatoes, halved
- 1/2 cucumber, diced
- 1/4 red onion, thinly sliced
- 1/4 cup Kalamata olives, halved
- 1/4 cup crumbled feta cheese
- 2 tablespoons capers, drained
- 2 tablespoons fresh parsley, chopped
- 3 tablespoons extra virgin olive oil
- 1 tablespoon lemon juice
- 1 teaspoon dried oregano
- Salt and pepper to taste

DIRECTIONS:

1. In a large bowl, combine the drained tuna, cherry tomatoes, cucumber, red onion, Kalamata olives, feta cheese, capers, and fresh parsley.
2. In a small bowl, whisk together the olive oil, lemon juice, dried oregano, salt, and pepper.
3. Pour the dressing over the salad ingredients and toss gently to combine.
4. Serve the salad immediately or refrigerate for 15-30 minutes to allow the flavors to meld together.

Roasted Beet Salad with Walnuts

 PREPARATION TIME: 15 MINUTES

 COOKING TIME: 45 MINUTES (roasting time)

 SERVES: 4

Nutrition Information (Per Serving):
200 Calories / 12g Fat / 20g Carbohydrates / 4g Protein / 150mg Sodium / 10g Sugar

INGREDIENTS:

- 4 medium beets, trimmed and scrubbed
- 1/2 cup walnuts, toasted
- 1/4 cup crumbled goat cheese or feta cheese (optional)
- 2 tablespoons fresh parsley, chopped
- 4 cups mixed salad greens (arugula, spinach, etc.)
- 2 tablespoons olive oil
- 1 tablespoon balsamic vinegar
- 1 teaspoon honey (optional)
- Salt and pepper to taste

DIRECTIONS:

1. Preheat your oven to 400°F (200°C). Wrap each beet in aluminum foil and place them on a baking sheet. Roast in the oven for 40-45 minutes, or until tender when pierced with a fork. Let the beets cool, then peel and cut them into wedges or slices.
2. In a small bowl, whisk together the olive oil, balsamic vinegar, honey (if using), salt, and pepper.
3. In a large bowl, combine the roasted beets, toasted walnuts, mixed salad greens, and chopped parsley. Drizzle with the dressing and toss gently to combine.
4. If desired, sprinkle with crumbled goat cheese or feta.
5. Serve the salad at room temperature.

Carrot and Cumin Soup

 PREPARATION TIME: 10 MINUTES

 COOKING TIME: 25 MINUTES

 SERVES: 4

Nutrition Information (Per Serving):
150 Calories / 7g Fat / 20g Carbohydrates / 2g Protein / 300mg Sodium / 8g Sugar

INGREDIENTS:

- 2 tablespoons olive oil
- 1 onion, chopped
- 2 garlic cloves, minced
- 1 teaspoon ground cumin
- 1 pound carrots, peeled and sliced
- 4 cups vegetable broth
- Salt and pepper to taste
- Fresh cilantro or parsley for garnish (optional)
- A squeeze of lemon juice (optional)

DIRECTIONS:

1. In a large pot, heat olive oil over medium heat. Add the chopped onion and sauté for 5-7 minutes until softened. Add the minced garlic and cumin, and cook for another 1-2 minutes until fragrant.
2. Add the sliced carrots to the pot and pour in the vegetable broth. Bring to a boil, then reduce the heat and simmer for about 20 minutes, until the carrots are tender.
3. Use an immersion blender to puree the soup until smooth, or transfer the soup to a blender and blend in batches. Return the soup to the pot.
4. Season with salt and pepper to taste. If desired, add a squeeze of lemon juice for extra brightness.
5. Serve the soup hot, garnished with fresh cilantro or parsley

Zucchini and Mint Soup

 PREPARATION TIME: 10 MINUTES

 COOKING TIME: 20 MINUTES

SERVES: 4

Nutrition Information (Per Serving):
120 Calories / 6g Fat / 12g Carbohydrates / 3g Protein / 250mg Sodium / 4g Sugar

INGREDIENTS:

- 2 tablespoons olive oil
- 1 onion, chopped
- 2 garlic cloves, minced
- 4 medium zucchinis, sliced
- 4 cups vegetable broth
- 1/4 cup fresh mint leaves, chopped
- Salt and pepper to taste
- Greek yogurt or sour cream for garnish (optional)

DIRECTIONS:

1. In a large pot, heat olive oil over medium heat. Add the chopped onion and sauté for 5-7 minutes until softened. Add the minced garlic and cook for another 1-2 minutes until fragrant.
2. Add the sliced zucchini to the pot and pour in the vegetable broth. Bring to a boil, then reduce the heat and simmer for about 15 minutes, until the zucchini is tender.
3. Use an immersion blender to puree the soup until smooth, or transfer the soup to a blender and blend in batches. Return the soup to the pot.
4. Stir in the chopped fresh mint and season with salt and pepper to taste.
5. Serve the soup hot, garnished with a dollop of Greek yogurt or sour cream if desired.

Chapter ④

VEGGIES and SIDE DISHES

Honey and Thyme Roasted Vegetables

PREPARATION TIME: 10 MINUTES

COOKING TIME: 35 MINUTES

SERVES: 4

Nutrition Information (Per Serving):
180 Calories / 9g Fat / 25g Carbohydrates / 3g Protein /
250mg Sodium / 10g Sugar

INGREDIENTS:

- 4 cups mixed vegetables (such as carrots, parsnips, sweet potatoes, and Brussels sprouts), cut into bite-sized pieces
- 2 tablespoons olive oil
- 2 tablespoons honey
- 1 tablespoon fresh thyme leaves (or 1 teaspoon dried thyme)
- Salt and pepper to taste
- 1 tablespoon balsamic vinegar (optional, for added flavor)

DIRECTIONS:

1. Preheat your oven to 400°F (200°C).
2. In a large bowl, combine the mixed vegetables, olive oil, honey, thyme, salt, and pepper. Toss until the vegetables are evenly coated.
3. Spread the vegetables in a single layer on a baking sheet lined with parchment paper.
4. Roast in the preheated oven for 30-35 minutes, or until the vegetables are tender and caramelized, stirring halfway through for even cooking.
5. If using, drizzle the roasted vegetables with balsamic vinegar and toss gently to combine.
6. Serve hot, as a delicious and flavorful side dish.

Lemon Garlic Quinoa

PREPARATION TIME: 5 MINUTES

COOKING TIME: 15 MINUTES

SERVES: 4

Nutrition Information (Per Serving):
160 Calories / 6g Fat / 24g Carbohydrates / 5g Protein /
150mg Sodium / 1g Sugar

INGREDIENTS:

- 1 cup quinoa, rinsed
- 2 cups vegetable broth or water
- 2 tablespoons olive oil
- 2 cloves garlic, minced
- Zest and juice of 1 lemon
- Salt and pepper to taste
- 2 tablespoons fresh parsley, chopped (optional, for garnish)

DIRECTIONS:

1. In a medium saucepan, combine the rinsed quinoa and vegetable broth or water. Bring to a boil over medium-high heat.
2. Reduce the heat to low, cover, and simmer for about 15 minutes, or until the quinoa is cooked and the liquid is absorbed. Remove from heat and let it sit, covered, for 5 minutes.
3. While the quinoa is cooking, heat the olive oil in a small skillet over medium heat. Add the minced garlic and sauté for 1-2 minutes until fragrant, being careful not to burn it.
4. Fluff the cooked quinoa with a fork and transfer it to a large bowl. Add the sautéed garlic, lemon zest, and lemon juice. Stir to combine.
5. Season with salt and pepper to taste.
6. Serve warm, garnished with chopped fresh parsley if desired.

Mediterranean Couscous

 PREPARATION TIME: 10 MINUTES

 COOKING TIME: 10 MINUTES

 SERVES: 4

Nutrition Information (Per Serving):
210 Calories / 7g Fat / 32g Carbohydrates / 6g Protein / 300mg Sodium / 2g Sugar

INGREDIENTS:

- 1 cup couscous
- 1 1/4 cups vegetable broth or water
- 2 tablespoons olive oil
- 1/2 cup cherry tomatoes, halved
- 1/2 cup cucumber, diced
- 1/4 cup Kalamata olives, sliced
- 1/4 cup red onion, finely chopped
- 1/4 cup crumbled feta cheese
- 2 tablespoons fresh parsley, chopped
- Juice of 1 lemon
- Salt and pepper to taste

DIRECTIONS:

1. In a medium saucepan, bring the vegetable broth or water to a boil. Stir in the couscous, cover, and remove from heat. Let it sit for 5 minutes, then fluff with a fork.
2. In a large bowl, combine the couscous with the cherry tomatoes, cucumber, Kalamata olives, red onion, and crumbled feta cheese.
3. Drizzle the olive oil and lemon juice over the couscous mixture. Toss to combine.
4. Season with salt and pepper to taste.
5. Garnish with fresh parsley and serve the couscous at room temperature or slightly chilled.

Simple Greek Rice Pilaf

 PREPARATION TIME: 5 MINUTES

 COOKING TIME: 20 MINUTES

 SERVES: 4

Nutrition Information (Per Serving):
180 Calories / 5g Fat / 30g Carbohydrates / 4g Protein / 300mg Sodium / 1g Sugar

INGREDIENTS:

- 1 cup long-grain rice (like basmati or jasmine)
- 2 cups vegetable broth or water
- 1 small onion, finely chopped
- 2 tablespoons olive oil
- 1 garlic clove, minced
- 1/4 teaspoon ground cinnamon (optional)
- 1/4 teaspoon ground allspice (optional)
- Salt and pepper to taste
- 2 tablespoons fresh parsley, chopped (for garnish)
- 1 tablespoon fresh lemon juice (optional, for a fresh zing)

DIRECTIONS:

1. In a large saucepan, heat the olive oil over medium heat. Add the chopped onion and sauté for about 3-4 minutes until softened.
2. Add the minced garlic and cook for another 1-2 minutes until fragrant.
3. Stir in the rice, coating it well with the olive oil, and cook for 2 minutes, allowing it to lightly toast.
4. Add the vegetable broth, cinnamon, and allspice (if using). Bring the mixture to a boil, then reduce the heat to low, cover, and simmer for about 15 minutes, or until the rice is cooked and the liquid is absorbed.
5. Remove the pan from heat and let it sit, covered, for 5 minutes. Fluff the rice with a fork.
6. Season with salt and pepper to taste, and stir in the fresh lemon juice, if using.
7. Garnish with chopped fresh parsley before serving.

Grilled Zucchini

 PREPARATION TIME: 5 MINUTES

 COOKING TIME: 10 MINUTES

SERVES: 4

Nutrition Information (Per Serving):
70 Calories / 5g Fat / 6g Carbohydrates / 1g Protein /
150mg Sodium / 3g Sugar

INGREDIENTS:

- 4 medium zucchinis, sliced lengthwise into 1/4-inch thick strips
- 2 tablespoons olive oil
- 1 teaspoon garlic powder or 2 cloves fresh garlic, minced
- Salt and pepper to taste
- 1 tablespoon fresh lemon juice (optional)
- 1 tablespoon fresh parsley or basil, chopped (for garnish)

DIRECTIONS:

1. Preheat your grill to medium-high heat.
2. In a large bowl, toss the zucchini slices with olive oil, garlic powder (or minced fresh garlic), salt, and pepper until evenly coated.
3. Place the zucchini slices on the grill and cook for 3-4 minutes on each side, until grill marks appear and the zucchini is tender but not mushy.
4. Remove the zucchini from the grill and drizzle with fresh lemon juice, if desired.
5. Garnish with chopped fresh parsley or basil before serving.

Garlic Roasted Cauliflower

 PREPARATION TIME: 10 MINUTES

 COOKING TIME: 25 MINUTES

 SERVES: 4

Nutrition Information (Per Serving):
120 Calories / 7g Fat / 12g Carbohydrates / 3g Protein /
200mg Sodium / 2g Sugar

INGREDIENTS:

- 1 large head of cauliflower, cut into florets
- 3 cloves garlic, minced
- 3 tablespoons olive oil
- 1 teaspoon smoked paprika (optional)
- Salt and pepper to taste
- 1 tablespoon fresh parsley, chopped (optional, for garnish)
- 1 tablespoon lemon juice (optional, for garnish)

DIRECTIONS:

1. Preheat your oven to 400°F (200°C).
2. In a large bowl, toss the cauliflower florets with olive oil, minced garlic, smoked paprika (if using), salt, and pepper until evenly coated.
3. Spread the cauliflower in a single layer on a baking sheet lined with parchment paper.
4. Roast in the preheated oven for 20-25 minutes, stirring halfway through, until the cauliflower is tender and golden brown.
5. Remove from the oven and drizzle with lemon juice, if desired. Garnish with chopped fresh parsley.

Lemon Potatoes

 PREPARATION TIME: 10 MINUTES

 COOKING TIME: 40 MINUTES

 SERVES: 4

Nutrition Information (Per Serving):
180 Calories / 9g Fat / 25g Carbohydrates / 3g Protein / 300mg Sodium / 2g Sugar

INGREDIENTS:

- 4 large potatoes, peeled and cut into wedges
- 1/4 cup olive oil
- Juice of 2 lemons
- 3 cloves garlic, minced
- 1 teaspoon dried oregano
- 1/2 teaspoon ground cumin (optional)
- 1/2 cup vegetable broth or water
- Salt and pepper to taste
- Fresh parsley, chopped (optional, for garnish)

DIRECTIONS:

1. Preheat your oven to 400°F (200°C).
2. In a large bowl, combine the potato wedges, olive oil, lemon juice, minced garlic, dried oregano, cumin (if using), salt, and pepper. Toss until the potatoes are evenly coated.
3. Place the potatoes in a single layer in a large baking dish.
4. Pour the vegetable broth or water around the potatoes in the dish.
5. Roast in the preheated oven for 40 minutes, stirring halfway through, until the potatoes are tender and golden brown.
6. Remove from the oven and garnish with chopped fresh parsley, if desired.

Spanakorizo (Spinach Rice)

 PREPARATION TIME: 10 MINUTES

 COOKING TIME: 25 MINUTES

 SERVES: 4

Nutrition Information (Per Serving):
180 Calories / 7g Fat / 28g Carbohydrates / 4g Protein / 300mg Sodium / 2g Sugar

INGREDIENTS:

- 1 cup long-grain rice (such as basmati or jasmine)
- 1 lb fresh spinach, roughly chopped
- 1 small onion, finely chopped
- 2 cloves garlic, minced
- 1/4 cup olive oil
- 1/4 cup fresh dill, chopped
- Juice of 1 lemon
- 2 cups vegetable broth or water
- Salt and pepper to taste
- Feta cheese, crumbled (optional, for garnish)

DIRECTIONS:

1. In a large pot, heat the olive oil over medium heat. Add the chopped onion and garlic, and sauté for about 3-4 minutes until softened.
2. Add the rice to the pot and stir to coat it with the olive oil. Cook for 2 minutes, allowing the rice to lightly toast.
3. Pour in the vegetable broth or water and bring to a boil. Reduce the heat to low, cover, and simmer for 10 minutes.
4. Add the chopped spinach and fresh dill to the pot. Stir well, cover, and cook for another 10-15 minutes, until the rice is fully cooked and the spinach is wilted.
5. Remove from heat, stir in the lemon juice, and season with salt and pepper to taste.
6. Serve warm, garnished with crumbled feta cheese if desired.

Dolmades (Stuffed Grape Leaves)

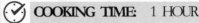 **PREPARATION TIME:** 30 MINUTES

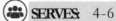 **COOKING TIME:** 1 HOUR

SERVES: 4-6

Nutrition Information (Per Serving):
150 Calories / 7g Fat / 20g Carbohydrates / 3g Protein / 350mg Sodium / 2g Sugar

INGREDIENTS:

- 1 jar (16 oz) grape leaves in brine, drained and rinsed
- 1 cup uncooked short-grain rice
- 1 small onion, finely chopped
- 2 cloves garlic, minced
- 1/4 cup pine nuts (optional)
- 1/4 cup raisins or currants (optional)
- 1/4 cup fresh parsley, chopped
- 2 tbsp fresh dill, chopped
- 2 tbsp fresh mint, chopped
- 1/4 cup olive oil, divided
- Juice of 2 lemons, divided
- 1 tsp ground cumin (optional)
- Salt and pepper to taste
- 2 cups water or vegetable broth

DIRECTIONS:

1. In a large skillet, heat 2 tablespoons of olive oil over medium heat. Add the chopped onion and garlic, and sauté for 3-4 minutes until softened.
2. Stir in the uncooked rice, pine nuts, and raisins or currants (if using). Cook for another 2 minutes, then remove from heat.
3. Add the fresh parsley, dill, mint, 1 tablespoon of lemon juice, cumin (if using), salt, and pepper to the rice mixture. Mix well.
4. Place a grape leaf on a flat surface, shiny side down. Add 1-2 teaspoons of the rice mixture near the stem end of the leaf. Fold in the sides and roll up tightly, like a burrito. Repeat with remaining leaves and filling.
5. Line the bottom of a large pot with a few grape leaves to prevent sticking. Arrange the stuffed grape leaves seam-side down in the pot, packing them snugly in layers.
6. Drizzle the remaining olive oil and lemon juice over the dolmades. Pour in enough water or vegetable broth to cover the dolmades. Place a heatproof plate on top to keep them from unrolling, and cover the pot.
7. Bring to a gentle simmer over low heat and cook for about 60 minutes, until the rice is tender.
8. After cooking, let the dolmades cool to room temperature. When ready to serve, they can be enjoyed cold, which is traditional, or gently warmed up if you prefer.

TIP: For the best flavor, make the dolmades a day ahead and let them chill in the refrigerator overnight. This allows the flavors to meld and intensify, making them even more delicious when served the next day.

Stuffed Bell Peppers (Vegetarian)

 PREPARATION TIME: 15 MINUTES

COOKING TIME: 35 MINUTES

SERVES: 4

Nutrition Information (Per Serving):
220 Calories / 8g Fat / 35g Carbohydrates / 6g Protein / 450mg Sodium / 5g Sugar

INGREDIENTS:

- 4 large bell peppers (any color), tops cut off and seeds removed
- 1 cup cooked rice (white, brown, or wild rice, as per your choice)
- 1 small onion, finely chopped
- 2 cloves garlic, minced
- 1 can (14.5 oz) diced tomatoes, drained
- 1/2 cup canned black beans or chickpeas, drained and rinsed
- 1/2 cup corn kernels (fresh, canned, or frozen)
- 1 teaspoon dried oregano
- 1 teaspoon dried basil
- 1/2 teaspoon ground cumin (optional)
- Salt and pepper to taste
- 1/2 cup shredded mozzarella or crumbled feta cheese (optional)
- 2 tablespoons olive oil
- Fresh parsley, chopped (for garnish)

DIRECTIONS:

1. Preheat your oven to 375°F (190°C).
2. In a large skillet, heat the olive oil over medium heat. Add the chopped onion and garlic, and sauté for 3-4 minutes until softened.
3. Stir in the cooked rice, diced tomatoes, black beans or chickpeas, corn, oregano, basil, cumin (if using), salt, and pepper. Cook for another 2-3 minutes until well combined and heated through.
4. Stuff each bell pepper with the rice mixture, pressing down lightly to pack it in.
5. Place the stuffed peppers upright in a baking dish. If using, sprinkle the tops with shredded mozzarella or crumbled feta cheese.
6. Cover the dish with aluminum foil and bake in the preheated oven for 25 minutes. Then, remove the foil and bake for an additional 10 minutes, until the peppers are tender and the cheese is melted and bubbly.
7. Garnish with chopped fresh parsley before serving.

TIP: If you're short on time, you can microwave the bell peppers for a few minutes before stuffing them. This will soften them up quickly, ensuring they cook through evenly in the oven without having to extend the baking time.

Grilled Asparagus with Lemon

 PREPARATION TIME: 5 MINUTES

 COOKING TIME: 10 MINUTES

SERVES: 4

Nutrition Information (Per Serving):
80 Calories / 7g Fat / 5g Carbohydrates / 2g Protein / 150mg Sodium / 2g Sugar

INGREDIENTS:

- 1 bunch of asparagus, trimmed
- 2 tablespoons olive oil
- 1 lemon (zested and juiced)
- 2 cloves garlic, minced
- Salt and pepper to taste
- 1 tablespoon grated Parmesan cheese (optional)
- Fresh parsley, chopped (optional, for garnish)

DIRECTIONS:

1. Preheat your grill to medium-high heat.
2. In a large bowl, toss the asparagus with olive oil, minced garlic, lemon zest, salt, and pepper until evenly coated.
3. Place the asparagus on the grill in a single layer and cook for 3-4 minutes on each side, until tender and slightly charred.
4. Remove the asparagus from the grill and drizzle with fresh lemon juice.
5. If desired, sprinkle with grated Parmesan cheese and garnish with chopped fresh parsley before serving.

Steamed Artichokes with Olive Oil

 PREPARATION TIME: 10 MINUTES

 COOKING TIME: 30-40 MINUTES

 SERVES: 4

Nutrition Information (Per Serving):
100 Calories / 7g Fat / 10g Carbohydrates / 2g Protein / 150mg Sodium / 1g Sugar

INGREDIENTS:

- 4 large artichokes
- 1/4 cup olive oil
- 2 cloves garlic, minced
- Juice of 1 lemon
- Salt and pepper to taste
- Fresh parsley, chopped (optional, for garnish)

DIRECTIONS:

1. Trim the stems of the artichokes to about 1 inch. Remove the tough outer leaves and snip off the sharp tips of the remaining leaves. Cut off the top inch of each artichoke.
2. Fill a large pot with about 2 inches of water and add a steaming basket. Place the artichokes in the basket, cover, and bring the water to a boil. Reduce the heat to a simmer and steam the artichokes for 30-40 minutes, or until the outer leaves pull away easily and the heart is tender.
3. In a small bowl, whisk together the olive oil, minced garlic, lemon juice, salt, and pepper.
4. Remove the artichokes from the pot and let them cool slightly. Drizzle the olive oil dressing over the artichokes.
5. Garnish with chopped fresh parsley if desired. Serve with an extra side of the olive oil dressing for dipping.

Marinated Olives

 PREPARATION TIME: 10 MINUTES

 COOKING TIME: 1-2 HOURS (or overnight for best flavor)

SERVES: 4-6

Nutrition Information (Per Serving):
150 Calories / 15g Fat / 2g Carbohydrates / 1g Protein / 300mg Sodium / 0g Sugar Ingredients:

INGREDIENTS:

- 2 cups mixed olives (green, black, Kalamata)
- 1/4 cup olive oil
- 2 cloves garlic, minced
- 1 teaspoon dried oregano
- 1 teaspoon dried thyme
- Zest of 1 lemon
- Juice of 1/2 lemon
- 1/2 teaspoon red pepper flakes (optional, for a bit of heat)
- 1 tablespoon fresh rosemary, chopped
- Salt and pepper to taste

DIRECTIONS:

1. In a large bowl, combine the olive oil, minced garlic, oregano, thyme, lemon zest, lemon juice, red pepper flakes (if using), and chopped rosemary.
2. Add the mixed olives to the bowl and toss until the olives are evenly coated with the marinade.
3. Cover and refrigerate the olives for at least 1-2 hours, or preferably overnight, to allow the flavors to meld.
4. Before serving, bring the olives to room temperature for the best flavor. Toss them again in the marinade and adjust seasoning with salt and pepper if needed.

Broccoli with Lemon and Garlic

 PREPARATION TIME: 5 MINUTES

 COOKING TIME: 10 MINUTES

 SERVES: 4

Nutrition Information (Per Serving):
90 Calories / 6g Fat / 9g Carbohydrates / 3g Protein / 120mg Sodium / 2g Sugar

INGREDIENTS:

- 1 large head of broccoli, cut into florets
- 2 tablespoons olive oil
- 3 cloves garlic, minced
- Zest and juice of 1 lemon
- Salt and pepper to taste
- Red pepper flakes (optional, for a bit of heat)
- Fresh parsley, chopped (optional, for garnish)

DIRECTIONS:

1. Steam the broccoli florets in a steamer basket over boiling water for 4-5 minutes, until just tender but still crisp.
2. While the broccoli is steaming, heat olive oil in a large skillet over medium heat. Add the minced garlic and sauté for 1-2 minutes until fragrant.
3. Add the steamed broccoli to the skillet and toss to coat in the garlic and olive oil. Cook for 2-3 minutes, stirring occasionally.
4. Remove from heat and add the lemon zest and juice. Season with salt, pepper, and red pepper flakes if using. Toss to combine.
5. Transfer to a serving dish and garnish with fresh parsley if desired.

Turkish Green Beans with Almonds

 PREPARATION TIME: 10 MINUTES

COOKING TIME: 25 MINUTES

SERVES: 4

Nutrition Information (Per Serving):
130 Calories / 8g Fat / 12g Carbohydrates / 3g Protein / 200mg Sodium / 3g Sugar

INGREDIENTS:

- 1 pound green beans, trimmed
- 2 tablespoons olive oil
- 1 small onion, finely chopped
- 3 cloves garlic, minced
- 1 large tomato, chopped
- 1/4 cup sliced almonds
- 1/2 teaspoon ground cumin
- Salt and pepper to taste
- Juice of 1/2 lemon
- Fresh parsley, chopped (optional, for garnish)

DIRECTIONS:

1. Heat olive oil in a large skillet over medium heat. Sauté the onion for 3-4 minutes until softened, then add garlic and cook for 1-2 minutes until fragrant.
2. Add the chopped tomato and cook for 5 minutes to create a sauce.
3. Stir in the green beans, cover, and cook for 15-20 minutes, stirring occasionally, until tender.
4. Toast the almonds in a small pan over medium heat for 2-3 minutes until golden.
5. Season the green beans with cumin, salt, and pepper. Drizzle with lemon juice, stir, and transfer to a serving dish.
6. Top with toasted almonds and garnish with fresh parsley if desired.

Caramelized Onions and Peppers

 PREPARATION TIME: 10 MINUTES

 COOKING TIME: 30 MINUTES

SERVES: 4

Nutrition Information (Per Serving):
150 Calories / 7g Fat / 20g Carbohydrates / 2g Protein / 200mg Sodium / 8g Sugar

INGREDIENTS:

- 2 large onions, thinly sliced
- 2 large bell peppers (any color), thinly sliced
- 2 tablespoons olive oil
- 1 tablespoon balsamic vinegar (optional)
- 1 teaspoon sugar (optional, for extra caramelization)
- Salt and pepper to taste
- Fresh thyme or basil for garnish (optional)

DIRECTIONS:

1. In a large skillet, heat the olive oil over medium heat.
2. Add the sliced onions to the skillet and cook, stirring occasionally, for about 10 minutes until the onions begin to soften and turn golden.
3. Add the sliced bell peppers to the skillet. Continue to cook, stirring occasionally, for another 15-20 minutes, until both the onions and peppers are deeply caramelized and tender.
4. If desired, stir in the balsamic vinegar and sugar for extra depth of flavor and enhanced caramelization. Cook for an additional 2-3 minutes.
5. Season with salt and pepper to taste.
6. Garnish with fresh thyme or basil if desired, and serve warm.

Farro with Mushrooms and Carrots

 PREPARATION TIME: 10 MINUTES

 COOKING TIME: 30 MINUTES

 SERVES: 4

Nutrition Information (Per Serving):
220 Calories / 7g Fat / 35g Carbohydrates / 6g Protein / 300mg Sodium / 4g Sugar

INGREDIENTS:

- 1 cup farro, rinsed
- 2 1/2 cups vegetable broth or water
- 2 tablespoons olive oil
- 1 small onion, finely chopped
- 2 cloves garlic, minced
- 1 cup mushrooms, sliced
- 2 carrots, peeled and diced
- 1 teaspoon dried thyme
- Salt and pepper to taste
- Fresh parsley, chopped (optional, for garnish)

DIRECTIONS:

1. In a medium saucepan, combine the rinsed farro and vegetable broth or water. Bring to a boil, then reduce the heat to low, cover, and simmer for 20-25 minutes until the farro is tender and the liquid is absorbed. Drain any excess liquid if needed.
2. While the farro is cooking, heat the olive oil in a large skillet over medium heat. Add the chopped onion and sauté for 3-4 minutes until softened.
3. Add the garlic, sliced mushrooms, and diced carrots to the skillet. Cook for 5-7 minutes until the vegetables are tender and the mushrooms have released their juices.
4. Stir in the cooked farro, dried thyme, salt, and pepper. Cook for an additional 2-3 minutes, stirring to combine the flavors.
5. Transfer to a serving dish and garnish with fresh parsley if desired.

Quick and Easy Pickled Vegetables

 PREPARATION TIME: 10 MINUTES

 COOKING TIME: 1 HOUR (or longer for more intense flavor)

 SERVES: 4

Nutrition Information (Per Serving):
40 Calories / 1g Fat / 8g Carbohydrates / 1g Protein / 400mg Sodium / 4g Sugar

INGREDIENTS:

- 1 cup each of red onions, beets, carrots, cucumbers, bell peppers, cauliflowers, thinly sliced (about 1/8-inch thick)
- 1 cup white vinegar, 1 cup water
- 2 tablespoons sugar, 1 tablespoon salt
- 1 teaspoon black peppercorns
- 1 teaspoon mustard seeds
- 1/2 teaspoon red pepper flakes (optional)
- 2 cloves garlic, smashed
- Fresh dill or other herbs (optional)

DIRECTIONS:

1. Place the sliced red onions, beets, carrots, cucumbers, bell peppers, cauliflowers, clean jar or container.
2. In a small saucepan, combine the vinegar, water, sugar, salt, black peppercorns, mustard seeds, red pepper flakes (if using), and garlic. Bring the mixture to a boil, stirring until the sugar and salt dissolve.
3. Pour the hot brine over the vegetables in the jar, ensuring they are fully submerged. Add fresh dill or other herbs if desired.
4. Let the jar cool to room temperature, then cover and refrigerate for at least 1 hour before serving. For the best flavor, allow the vegetables to marinate for several hours or overnight.
5. Enjoy these pickled vegetables as a tangy side dish, snack, or topping for sandwiches and salads.

Sweet Potatoes with Hummus and Chickpeas

PREPARATION TIME: 10 MINUTES

COOKING TIME: 40 MINUTES

SERVES: 4

Nutrition Information (Per Serving):
300 Calories / 12g Fat / 42g Carbohydrates / 8g Protein / 350mg Sodium / 9g Sugar

INGREDIENTS:

- 4 medium sweet potatoes, scrubbed and pierced with a fork
- 1 cup hummus (see recipe on p.21)
- 1 can (15 oz) chickpeas, drained and rinsed
- 1 tablespoon olive oil
- 1 teaspoon ground cumin
- 1/2 teaspoon smoked paprika (optional)
- Salt and pepper to taste
- Fresh parsley, chopped (optional, for garnish)

DIRECTIONS:

1. Preheat the oven to 400°F (200°C). Bake the pierced sweet potatoes for 35-40 minutes, until tender.
2. While the sweet potatoes bake, heat olive oil in a skillet over medium heat. Add chickpeas, cumin, smoked paprika (if using), salt, and pepper. Cook for 5-7 minutes, stirring occasionally, until chickpeas are warm and slightly crispy.
3. Slice the baked sweet potatoes open lengthwise and fluff the insides with a fork. Add hummus to each sweet potato.
4. Top with the seasoned chickpeas.
5. Garnish with parsley.

Eggplant Parmesan (Lighter Version)

PREPARATION TIME: 20 MINUTES

COOKING TIME: 40 MINUTES

SERVES: 4

Nutrition Information (Per Serving):
320 Calories / 18g Fat / 24g Carbohydrates / 12g Protein / 700mg Sodium / 8g Sugar

INGREDIENTS:

- 2 large eggplants, sliced into 1/2-inch rounds
- 1 cup marinara sauce
- 1 cup shredded mozzarella cheese
- 1/2 cup grated Parmesan cheese
- 1 tablespoon olive oil
- Salt and pepper to taste
- Fresh basil, chopped (optional)

DIRECTIONS:

1. Preheat your oven to 375°F (190°C). Arrange the eggplant slices on a baking sheet and brush both sides with olive oil. Season with salt and pepper.
2. Bake the eggplant for 20 minutes, flipping halfway through, until tender.
3. Spread a thin layer of marinara sauce in a baking dish. Layer the baked eggplant slices on top.
4. Sprinkle with mozzarella and Parmesan cheese, then add another layer of marinara sauce. Repeat the layers until all the ingredients are used.
5. Bake for 20 minutes, until the cheese is melted and bubbly. Garnish with fresh basil if desired.

Chapter 5

FISH and SEAFOOD

Grilled Salmon with Dill

PREPARATION TIME: 10 MINUTES

MARINATING TIME: 15-30 MINUTES

COOKING TIME: 10-12 MINUTES

SERVES: 4

Nutrition Information (Per Serving):
320 Calories / 18g Fat / 2g Carbohydrates / 34g Protein /
90mg Sodium / 1g Sugar

INGREDIENTS:

- 4 salmon fillets (about 6 oz each)
- 2 tablespoons olive oil
- Juice of 1 lemon
- 2 tablespoons fresh dill, chopped (or 1 tablespoon dried dill)
- 2 cloves garlic, minced
- Salt and pepper to taste
- Lemon wedges, for serving
- Fresh dill sprigs, for garnish (optional)

DIRECTIONS:

1. Mix olive oil, lemon juice, dill, garlic, salt, and pepper in a bowl.
2. Marinate salmon fillets in the mixture for 15-30 minutes.
3. Preheat the grill to medium-high heat (375°F to 400°F).
4. Oil the grill grates, then grill the salmon skin-side down for 4-6 minutes per side, until cooked through.
5. Serve with lemon wedges and garnish with fresh dill.

TIP: Serve the salmon with a side of grilled vegetables or a light salad for a complete Mediterranean meal.

Simple Shrimp Scampi

PREPARATION TIME: 10 MINUTES

COOKING TIME: 10 MINUTES

SERVES: 4

Nutrition Information (Per Serving):
310 Calories / 18g Fat / 7g Carbohydrates / 24g Protein /
400mg Sodium / 1g Sugar

INGREDIENTS:

- 1 lb large shrimp, peeled and deveined
- 3 tablespoons olive oil
- 4 cloves garlic, minced
- 1/4 teaspoon red pepper flakes (optional)
- 1/2 cup dry white wine (or chicken broth)
- Juice of 1 lemon
- 3 tablespoons unsalted butter
- Salt and pepper to taste
- 2 tablespoons fresh parsley, chopped
- 8 oz linguine or spaghetti (optional)
- Lemon wedges, for serving

DIRECTIONS:

1. Cook the pasta according to package instructions if using. Drain and set aside.
2. Heat olive oil in a large skillet over medium-high heat. Add shrimp and cook for 1-2 minutes per side, until pink and opaque. Remove shrimp and set aside.
3. In the same skillet, add garlic and red pepper flakes. Sauté for 30 seconds until fragrant. Add white wine and lemon juice, simmer for 2-3 minutes.
4. Stir in butter until melted. Return shrimp to the skillet and toss to coat in the sauce. Season with salt and pepper.
5. Serve immediately, garnished with fresh parsley and lemon wedges. Toss with pasta if desired.

Baked Cod with Lemon

 PREPARATION TIME: 10 MINUTES

 COOKING TIME: 15-20 MINUTES

 SERVES: 4

Nutrition Information (Per Serving):
220 Calories / 9g Fat / 2g Carbohydrates / 32g Protein / 180mg Sodium / 1g Sugar

INGREDIENTS:

- 4 cod fillets (about 6 oz each)
- 2 tablespoons olive oil
- Juice of 1 lemon
- Zest of 1 lemon
- 2 cloves garlic, minced
- 1 teaspoon dried oregano
- Salt and pepper to taste
- Fresh parsley, chopped (optional, for garnish)
- Lemon wedges, for serving

DIRECTIONS:

1. Preheat the oven to 400°F (200°C). Line a baking sheet with parchment paper or lightly grease it.
2. In a small bowl, mix together olive oil, lemon juice, lemon zest, garlic, oregano, salt, and pepper.
3. Place the cod fillets on the prepared baking sheet. Brush the lemon mixture over the fillets, ensuring they are evenly coated.
4. Bake in the preheated oven for 15-20 minutes, or until the cod is opaque and flakes easily with a fork.
5. Serve immediately, garnished with fresh parsley and lemon wedges.

TIP: Pair the baked cod with a Greek salad, roasted vegetables, or herb-roasted potatoes.

Mussels in White Wine Sauce

 PREPARATION TIME: 10 MINUTES

 COOKING TIME: 10 MINUTES

 SERVES: 4

Nutrition Information (Per Serving):
250 Calories / 10g Fat / 6g Carbohydrates / 30g Protein / 500mg Sodium / 1g Sugar

INGREDIENTS:

- 2 lbs fresh mussels, scrubbed and with beards removed
- 2 tablespoons olive oil
- 4 cloves garlic, minced
- 1 small shallot, finely chopped
- 1 cup dry white wine
- 1/2 cup vegetable or fish broth
- Juice of 1 lemon
- 2 tablespoons unsalted butter
- Salt and pepper to taste
- Fresh parsley, chopped (optional, for garnish)
- Crusty bread, for serving

DIRECTIONS:

1. Heat olive oil in a large, deep skillet or pot over medium heat. Add the minced garlic and chopped shallot, sautéing for 2-3 minutes until softened and fragrant.
2. Pour in the white wine and broth, bringing the mixture to a simmer. Cook for 2 minutes to allow the flavors to meld.
3. Add the cleaned mussels to the skillet, cover, and cook for 5-7 minutes, shaking the pan occasionally, until the mussels have opened. Discard any mussels that do not open.
4. Stir in the lemon juice and butter, allowing the butter to melt into the sauce. Season with salt and pepper to taste.
5. Serve immediately, garnished with fresh parsley and accompanied by crusty bread to soak up the delicious sauce.

Mediterranean Tuna Steaks

⚒ **PREPARATION TIME:** 10 MINUTES

🍲 **MARINATING TIME:** 15 MINUTES

⏱ **COOKING TIME:** 6-8 MINUTES

👥 **SERVES:** 4

Nutrition Information (Per Serving):
300 Calories / 15g Fat / 2g Carbohydrates / 38g Protein /
350mg Sodium / 1g Sugar

INGREDIENTS:

- 4 tuna steaks (about 6 oz each)
- 2 tablespoons olive oil
- 2 cloves garlic, minced
- 1 teaspoon dried oregano
- 1 teaspoon dried thyme
- Juice and zest of 1 lemon
- 1/4 cup Kalamata olives, pitted and halved
- 1/4 cup sun-dried tomatoes, chopped
- Salt and pepper to taste
- Fresh parsley, chopped (for garnish)
- Lemon wedges (for serving)

DIRECTIONS:

1. In a small bowl, combine the olive oil, minced garlic, dried oregano, dried thyme, lemon juice, and lemon zest. Mix well. Pat the tuna steaks dry with a paper towel and season both sides with salt and pepper. Brush the lemon-herb mixture over both sides of the tuna steaks, ensuring they are evenly coated. Let the tuna steaks marinate for 15 minutes.
2. Heat a large skillet or grill pan over medium-high heat. Once hot, add the tuna steaks and cook for 2-3 minutes per side, or until they reach your desired level of doneness (tuna is best served slightly pink in the center).
3. In the last minute of cooking, add the Kalamata olives and sun-dried tomatoes to the pan to warm them slightly.
4. Remove the tuna steaks from the pan and let them rest for a minute before serving.
5. Garnish the tuna steaks with fresh parsley and serve with lemon wedges on the side.

Lemon Herb Tilapia

⚒ **PREPARATION TIME:** 10 MINUTES

🍲 **MARINATING TIME:** 10 -15MINUTES (optional but recommended)

⏱ **COOKING TIME:** 10 -12 MINUTES

👥 **SERVES:** 4

Nutrition Information (Per Serving):
230 Calories / 11g Fat / 2g Carbohydrates / 30g Protein /
240mg Sodium / 0g Sugar

INGREDIENTS:

- 4 tilapia fillets (about 6 oz each)
- 2 tablespoons olive oil
- Juice and zest of 1 lemon
- 2 cloves garlic, minced
- 1 teaspoon dried thyme
- 1 teaspoon dried oregano
- Salt and pepper to taste
- Fresh parsley, chopped (optional, for garnish)
- Lemon wedges, for serving

DIRECTIONS:

1. Preheat the oven to 400°F (200°C). Lightly grease a baking dish or line it with parchment paper.
2. In a small bowl, mix together the olive oil, lemon juice, lemon zest, garlic, thyme, oregano, salt, and pepper.
3. Place the tilapia fillets in the prepared baking dish. Brush the lemon herb mixture over the fillets, ensuring they are evenly coated. Allow the fillets to marinate for 10-15 minutes for better flavor.
4. Place the baking dish in the preheated oven and bake for 10-12 minutes, or until the tilapia is opaque and flakes easily with a fork.
5. Remove from the oven and serve immediately. Garnish with fresh parsley and lemon wedges on the side.

Grilled Swordfish

⚒	**PREPARATION TIME:**	10 MINUTES
🍲	**MARINATING TIME:**	15 - 30 MINUTES
⏱	**COOKING TIME:**	8-10 MINUTES
👥	**SERVES:**	4

Nutrition Information (Per Serving):
320 Calories / 14g Fat / 1g Carbohydrates / 44g Protein / 220mg Sodium / 0g Sugar

INGREDIENTS:

- 4 swordfish steaks (about 6 oz each)
- 2 tablespoons olive oil
- Juice of 1 lemon
- 2 cloves garlic, minced
- 1 teaspoon dried oregano
- 1 teaspoon dried thyme
- Salt and pepper to taste
- Fresh parsley or basil, chopped (optional, for garnish)
- Lemon wedges, for serving

DIRECTIONS:

1. In a small bowl, mix together olive oil, lemon juice, garlic, oregano, thyme, salt, and pepper.
2. Rub the mixture over both sides of the swordfish steaks. Let them marinate for 15-30 minutes.
3. Preheat the grill to medium-high heat.
4. Grill the swordfish steaks for 4-5 minutes per side, or until the fish is opaque and has nice grill marks.
5. Serve immediately, garnished with fresh parsley or basil, and lemon wedges on the side.

TIP: Pair this dish with grilled vegetables, a fresh Greek salad, or herbed couscous.

Mediterranean Fish Stew

⚒	**PREPARATION TIME:**	15 MINUTES
⏱	**COOKING TIME:**	30 MINUTES
👥	**SERVES:**	4 -6

Nutrition Information (Per Serving):
280 Calories / 10g Fat / 15g Carbohydrates / 30g Protein / 600mg Sodium / 6g Sugar

INGREDIENTS:

- 1 lb firm white fish (cod, halibut, or sea bass), of your choice, cut into 1-inch pieces
- 2 tablespoons olive oil
- 1 onion, chopped; 2 cloves garlic, minced
- 1 red bell pepper, chopped
- 1 can (14.5 oz) diced tomatoes
- 1/4 cup dry white wine (optional)
- 2 cups vegetable or fish broth
- 1 teaspoon dried oregano, 1 teaspoon smoked paprika, 1/4 teaspoon red pepper flakes (optional)
- Salt and pepper to taste
- 1/4 cup fresh parsley, chopped
- Juice of 1 lemon
- Fresh basil or parsley for garnish

DIRECTIONS:

1. Heat the olive oil in a large pot over medium heat. Add the chopped onion, garlic, and red bell pepper. Sauté for 5-7 minutes, until the vegetables are softened.
2. Add the diced tomatoes (with their juice), white wine (if using), broth, oregano, smoked paprika, red pepper flakes (if using), salt, and pepper. Stir to combine and bring to a simmer.
3. Gently add the fish pieces to the simmering stew. Cover and cook for 10-12 minutes, or until the fish is opaque and flakes easily with a fork.
1. Stir in the chopped parsley and lemon juice. Taste and adjust the seasoning as needed.
2. Ladle the stew into bowls and garnish with fresh basil or parsley. Serve with crusty bread for soaking up the flavorful broth (optional).

Psari Plaki (Greek Baked Fish)

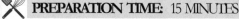
PREPARATION TIME: 15 MINUTES

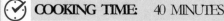
COOKING TIME: 40 MINUTES

SERVES: 4

Nutrition Information (Per Serving):
280 Calories / 12g Fat / 8g Carbohydrates / 32g Protein / 400mg Sodium / 4g Sugar

INGREDIENTS:

- 1.5 lbs white fish fillets (cod, haddock, or sea bass) of your choice
- 3 tablespoons olive oil
- 1 large onion, thinly sliced
- 3 cloves garlic, minced
- 1 can (14.5 oz) diced tomatoes
- 1/2 cup dry white wine (optional)
- Juice of 1 lemon
- 1 teaspoon dried oregano
- 1 teaspoon dried thyme
- Salt and pepper to taste
- 1/4 cup fresh parsley, chopped
- Lemon slices and fresh parsley for garnish (optional)

DIRECTIONS:

1. Preheat your oven to 375°F (190°C).
2. Heat 2 tablespoons of olive oil in a skillet over medium heat. Sauté the onion for 5-7 minutes until softened. Add garlic and cook for 1 minute.
3. Stir in diced tomatoes, white wine (if using), oregano, thyme, salt, and pepper. Simmer for 10 minutes.
4. Lightly grease a baking dish with the remaining olive oil. Place fish fillets in the dish, season with salt, pepper, and lemon juice.
5. Pour the tomato mixture over the fish. Bake for 25-30 minutes, or until the fish is opaque and flakes easily.
6. Serve with a garnish of fresh parsley and lemon slices, if desired.

Garlic Butter Scallops

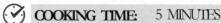
PREPARATION TIME: 10 MINUTES

COOKING TIME: 5 MINUTES

SERVES: 4

Nutrition Information (Per Serving):
220 Calories / 15g Fat / 6g Carbohydrates / 18g Protein / 400mg Sodium / 0g Sugar

INGREDIENTS:

- 1 lb large scallops, patted dry
- 3 tablespoons unsalted butter
- 4 cloves garlic, minced
- 2 tablespoons olive oil
- Juice of 1/2 lemon
- Salt and pepper to taste
- Fresh parsley, chopped (optional, for garnish)
- Lemon wedges, for serving

DIRECTIONS:

1. Season the scallops with salt and pepper on both sides.
2. Heat 2 tablespoons of butter and the olive oil in a large skillet over medium-high heat. Add the scallops in a single layer and cook for 2-3 minutes on each side, until golden brown and opaque. Remove the scallops from the skillet and set aside.
3. In the same skillet, add the remaining tablespoon of butter and the minced garlic. Sauté for 1 minute until fragrant.
4. Add the lemon juice and stir to combine. Return the scallops to the skillet, tossing them in the garlic butter sauce to coat.
5. Serve immediately, garnished with fresh parsley and lemon wedges.

TIP: Pair these scallops with a light salad, steamed vegetables, or a side of your choice of pasta.

Grilled Octopus

⚔ **PREPARATION TIME:**   15 MINUTES

🍲 **MARINATING TIME:**   15 MINUTES

⏱ **COOKING TIME:**   1 HOURS   (plus grilling time)

👥 **SERVES:**   4

Nutrition Information (Per Serving):
250 Calories / 12g Fat / 4g Carbohydrates / 30g Protein / 320mg Sodium / 0g Sugar

INGREDIENTS:

- 2-3 lbs octopus, cleaned
- 3 tablespoons olive oil
- Juice of 1 lemon
- 2 cloves garlic, minced
- 1 teaspoon dried oregano
- 1 bay leaf
- Salt and pepper to taste
- Fresh parsley, chopped (optional, for garnish)
- Lemon wedges, for serving

DIRECTIONS:

1. Bring a large pot of water to a boil. Add the bay leaf and a pinch of salt. Submerge the octopus and simmer for 45-60 minutes until tender. Drain and let cool slightly.
2. In a bowl, mix olive oil, lemon juice, garlic, oregano, salt, and pepper. Cut the octopus into large pieces, then toss in the marinade. Let sit for 15 minutes.
3. Preheat the grill to medium-high heat. Grill the octopus pieces for 3-4 minutes per side, until slightly charred and heated through.
4. Serve with a garnish of fresh parsley and lemon wedges.

Baked Sea Bass with Tomatoes

⚔ **PREPARATION TIME:**   10 MINUTES

⏱ **COOKING TIME:**   25-30 MINUTES

👥 **SERVES:**   4

Nutrition Information (Per Serving):
280 Calories / 12g Fat / 4g Carbohydrates / 36g Protein / 350mg Sodium / 3g Sugar

INGREDIENTS:

- 4 sea bass fillets (about 6 oz each)
- 2 tablespoons olive oil
- 2 cups cherry tomatoes, halved
- 2 cloves garlic, minced
- 1/4 cup Kalamata olives, pitted and halved (optional)
- 1/4 cup dry white wine (optional)
- 1 teaspoon dried oregano
- 1 teaspoon dried thyme
- Juice of 1 lemon
- Salt and pepper to taste
- Fresh basil or parsley, chopped (optional, for garnish)
- Lemon wedges, for serving

DIRECTIONS:

1. Preheat your oven to 400°F (200°C). Lightly grease a baking dish with olive oil.
2. Place the sea bass fillets in the baking dish. Season with salt, pepper, and lemon juice.
3. In a small bowl, mix together the cherry tomatoes, garlic, olives, white wine (if using), oregano, and thyme. Spoon this mixture over and around the sea bass fillets.
4. Bake in the preheated oven for 25-30 minutes, or until the sea bass is opaque and flakes easily with a fork.
5. Serve the sea bass topped with the baked tomatoes and garnished with fresh basil or parsley. Serve with lemon wedges on the side.

Baked Shrimp with Tomatos and Feta

 PREPARATION TIME: 10 MINUTES

 COOKING TIME: 15-20 MINUTES

SERVES: 4

Nutrition Information (Per Serving):
290 Calories / 15g Fat / 6g Carbohydrates / 30g Protein / 480mg Sodium / 3g Sugar

INGREDIENTS:

- 1 lb large shrimp, peeled and deveined
- 2 tablespoons olive oil
- 3 cloves garlic, minced
- 1 can (14.5 oz) diced tomatoes
- 1/4 cup dry white wine (optional)
- 1 teaspoon dried oregano
- 1/2 teaspoon red pepper flakes (optional)
- Salt and pepper to taste
- 1/2 cup crumbled feta cheese
- 2 tablespoons fresh parsley, chopped (optional, for garnish)
- Lemon wedges, for serving

DIRECTIONS:

1. Preheat your oven to 375°F (190°C). Lightly grease a baking dish with olive oil.
2. In a skillet, heat the olive oil over medium heat. Add the minced garlic and sauté for 1 minute until fragrant.
3. Add the diced tomatoes (with their juice), white wine (if using), oregano, red pepper flakes (if using), salt, and pepper. Simmer for 5 minutes, allowing the flavors to meld.
4. Arrange the shrimp in the baking dish. Pour the tomato mixture over the shrimp, then sprinkle the crumbled feta cheese on top.
5. Bake in the preheated oven for 15-20 minutes, or until the shrimp are pink and opaque, and the feta is slightly melted.
6. Serve immediately, garnished with fresh parsley and lemon wedges.

Calamari with Lemon and Garlic

 PREPARATION TIME: 10 MINUTES

 COOKING TIME: 5 MINUTES

SERVES: 4

Nutrition Information (Per Serving):
200 Calories / 10g Fat / 4g Carbohydrates / 22g Protein / 380mg Sodium / 1g Sugar

INGREDIENTS:

- 1 lb calamari, cleaned and cut into rings
- 3 tablespoons olive oil
- 3 cloves garlic, minced
- Juice of 1 lemon
- 1 teaspoon dried oregano
- Salt and pepper to taste
- Fresh parsley, chopped (optional, for garnish)
- Lemon wedges, for serving

DIRECTIONS:

1. Heat the olive oil in a large skillet over medium-high heat. Add the minced garlic and sauté for 1 minute until fragrant.
2. Add the calamari rings to the skillet. Cook for 2-3 minutes, stirring frequently, until the calamari is opaque and tender.
3. Stir in the lemon juice, oregano, salt, and pepper. Cook for an additional 1-2 minutes to combine the flavors.
4. Serve immediately, garnished with fresh parsley and lemon wedges on the side.

TIP: Serve this dish with a side of fresh salad, grilled vegetables, or a light pasta.

Salmon Lasagna

 PREPARATION TIME: 20 MINUTES

 COOKING TIME: 40 MINUTES

SERVES: 4

Nutrition Information (Per Serving):
450 Calories / 22g Fat / 35g Carbohydrates / 30g Protein / 800mg Sodium / 6g Sugar

INGREDIENTS:
- 12 lasagna noodles, cooked according to package instructions
- 1 lb salmon fillets, cooked and flaked
- 2 cups ricotta cheese
- 2 cups shredded mozzarella cheese
- 1/2 cup grated Parmesan cheese
- 2 cups fresh spinach, chopped
- 2 cloves garlic, minced
- 2 cups marinara sauce
- 1/2 cup heavy cream or half-and-half
- 1 tablespoon olive oil
- Salt and pepper to taste
- Fresh basil or parsley, chopped (optional, for garnish)

DIRECTIONS:
1. Preheat the oven to 375°F (190°C). Grease a 9x13-inch baking dish.
2. Mix ricotta, spinach, garlic, salt, pepper, and half the Parmesan in a bowl.
3. Spread a thin layer of marinara in the dish, then layer with noodles, ricotta mixture, and salmon. Drizzle with heavy cream. Repeat layers.
4. Top with noodles, remaining marinara, mozzarella, and Parmesan.
5. Cover with foil and bake for 30 minutes. Uncover and bake for 10 more minutes until cheese is bubbly.
6. Let cool slightly before serving. Garnish with fresh basil or parsley if desired.

Kalamaria Gemista (Stuffed Squid)

 PREPARATION TIME: 20 MINUTES

 COOKING TIME: 40 MINUTES

SERVES: 4

Nutrition Information (Per Serving):
350 Calories / 14g Fat / 30g Carbohydrates / 26g Protein / 600mg Sodium / 3g Sugar

INGREDIENTS:
- 1.5 lbs squid (8-10 medium), cleaned
- 1/2 cup uncooked rice
- 1 onion, finely chopped
- 3 cloves garlic, minced
- 1/4 cup olive oil
- 1/2 cup diced tomatoes
- 1/4 cup parsley, chopped
- 1 teaspoon dried oregano
- 1/2 teaspoon ground cinnamon (optional)
- 1/4 cup pine nuts (optional)
- Salt and pepper to taste
- 1/2 cup dry white wine (optional);
- 1/2 cup water or vegetable broth
- Lemon wedges, for serving

DIRECTIONS:
1. Preheat the oven to 375°F (190°C).
2. Heat 2 tablespoons of olive oil in a skillet over medium heat. Sauté the onion and garlic for 5 minutes until softened. Stir in rice, tomatoes, parsley, oregano, cinnamon, pine nuts, salt, and pepper. Cook for 2-3 minutes.
3. Stuff the squid with the rice mixture, leaving room for the rice to expand. Secure the ends with toothpicks.
4. Heat the remaining olive oil in the skillet. Brown the stuffed squid on each side for 2-3 minutes.
5. Transfer the squid to a baking dish. Pour the white wine (if using) and broth over the squid. Cover with foil and bake for 30-35 minutes until the squid is tender and the rice is cooked.
6. Serve hot with lemon wedges.

Sardines with Lemon and Herbs

 PREPARATION TIME: 10 MINUTES

 COOKING TIME: 10 MINUTES

SERVES: 4

Nutrition Information (Per Serving):
180 Calories / 10g Fat / 2g Carbohydrates / 20g Protein / 250mg Sodium / 1g Sugar

INGREDIENTS:

- 1 lb fresh sardines, cleaned and gutted
- 2 tablespoons olive oil
- Juice and zest of 1 lemon
- 2 cloves garlic, minced
- 1 teaspoon dried oregano
- 1 teaspoon dried thyme
- Salt and pepper to taste
- Fresh parsley, chopped (for garnish)
- Lemon wedges, for serving

DIRECTIONS:

1. Preheat your grill or broiler to medium-high heat.
2. In a small bowl, mix olive oil, lemon juice, lemon zest, garlic, oregano, thyme, salt, and pepper.
3. Brush the sardines with the lemon herb mixture on both sides.
4. Grill or broil the sardines for 3-4 minutes on each side, until they are cooked through and slightly charred.
5. Serve immediately, garnished with fresh parsley and lemon wedges.

TIP: Serve these sardines with a side of grilled vegetables or a light salad.

Salmon Patties

 PREPARATION TIME: 10 MINUTES

 COOKING TIME: 10 MINUTES

SERVES: 4

Nutrition Information (Per Serving):
250 Calories / 14g Fat / 8g Carbohydrates / 22g Protein / 350mg Sodium / 1g Sugar

INGREDIENTS:

- 1 can (14.75 oz) salmon, drained and flaked
- 1/2 cup breadcrumbs
- 1/4 cup finely chopped onion
- 1 egg, beaten
- 2 tablespoons fresh parsley, chopped
- 1 tablespoon mayonnaise
- 1 tablespoon Dijon mustard
- 1/2 teaspoon garlic powder
- Salt and pepper to taste
- 2 tablespoons olive oil (for frying)
- Lemon wedges, for serving

DIRECTIONS:

1. In a large bowl, combine the salmon, breadcrumbs, onion, egg, parsley, mayonnaise, Dijon mustard, garlic powder, salt, and pepper. Mix until well combined.
2. Form the mixture into 4 patties.
3. Heat the olive oil in a skillet over medium heat. Cook the patties for 3-4 minutes on each side, or until golden brown and cooked through.
4. Serve hot with lemon wedges.

TIP: These salmon patties are also delicious in a sandwich with fresh greens and a dollop of Tzatziki Dip.

Spanish Seafood Paella

 PREPARATION TIME: 15 MINUTES

 COOKING TIME: 45 MINUTES

 SERVES: 4

Nutrition Information (Per Serving):
420 Calories / 15g Fat / 46g Carbohydrates / 28g Protein / 780mg Sodium / 3g Sugar

INGREDIENTS:

- 2 tablespoons olive oil
- 1 onion, finely chopped
- 3 cloves garlic, minced
- 1 red bell pepper, chopped
- 1 yellow bell pepper, chopped
- 1 1/2 cups paella rice (Bomba or Arborio)
- 1/2 teaspoon smoked paprika
- 1/4 teaspoon saffron threads (soaked in 2 tablespoons of warm water)
- 1/2 teaspoon turmeric (optional, for color)
- 1/2 cup dry white wine
- 4 cups fish broth (or chicken broth)
- 1/2 lb large shrimp, peeled and deveined
- 1/2 lb mussels, cleaned and debearded
- 1/2 lb squid rings
- 1/2 cup frozen peas
- 1/2 cup chopped fresh parsley
- Salt and pepper to taste
- Lemon wedges, for serving

DIRECTIONS:

1. Heat the olive oil in a large pan or paella pan over medium heat. Add the chopped onion, garlic, and bell peppers. Cook for 5-7 minutes, until the vegetables are softened.
2. Stir in the paella rice, smoked paprika, and turmeric. Cook for 2 minutes, stirring constantly to coat the rice with the oil and spices.
3. Pour in the white wine and let it simmer for 2-3 minutes, allowing the alcohol to evaporate. Add the broth and the saffron with its soaking liquid. Stir everything together.
4. Reduce the heat to medium-low and let the rice cook for about 10 minutes, without stirring. Add the shrimp, mussels, and squid rings on top of the rice. Cover the pan with a lid or aluminum foil and cook for another 10-15 minutes, until the seafood is cooked through and the rice is tender.
5. During the last 5 minutes of cooking, sprinkle the peas over the top. Check for seasoning and add salt and pepper if needed.
6. Remove the pan from the heat and let it rest for 5 minutes. Garnish with fresh parsley and lemon wedges. Serve the paella directly from the pan.

TIP: A traditional paella pan is wide and flat, allowing the rice to cook evenly and develop that perfect "socarrat" (the crispy layer at the bottom). If you don't have a paella pan, use a large, flat skillet with a similar shape. Avoid using deep pots, as they prevent even cooking and can result in mushy rice.

Chapter (6)

MEAT and POULTRY

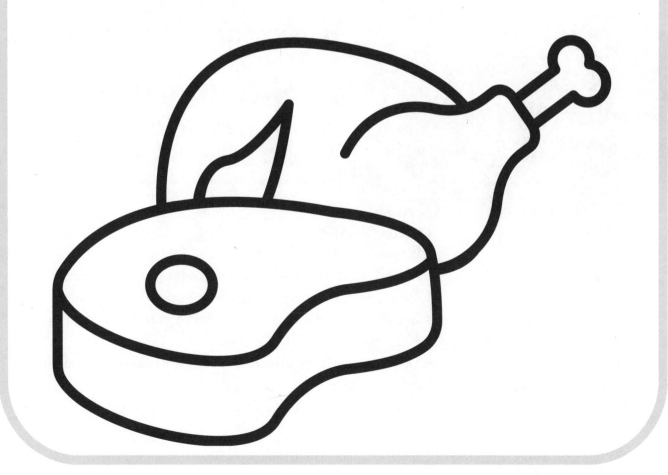

Spinach and Feta Stuffed Chicken

 PREPARATION TIME: 15 MINUTES

 COOKING TIME: 25-30 MINUTES

 SERVES: 4

Nutrition Information (Per Serving):
320 Calories / 15g Fat / 3g Carbohydrates / 40g Protein / 480mg Sodium / 1g Sugar

INGREDIENTS:

- 4 boneless, skinless chicken breasts
- 1 cup fresh spinach, chopped
- 1/2 cup feta cheese, crumbled
- 2 cloves garlic, minced
- 1 tablespoon olive oil
- 1 teaspoon dried oregano
- Salt and pepper to taste
- Toothpicks or kitchen twine (for securing the chicken)
- Lemon wedges, for serving

DIRECTIONS:

1. Preheat the oven to 375°F (190°C). Grease a baking dish.
2. In a bowl, mix the spinach, feta, garlic, olive oil, oregano, salt, and pepper.
3. Place each chicken breast flat on a cutting board. Holding the knife parallel to the board, carefully cut a deep pocket into the side of the chicken breast, being careful not to cut all the way through. The pocket should be large enough to hold the spinach and feta mixture. Stuff the pocket and secure with toothpicks or twine.
4. Sear the chicken in an ovenproof skillet over medium heat for 2-3 minutes per side until golden.
5. Transfer the skillet to the oven and bake for 20-25 minutes, or until the chicken is cooked through.
6. Let the chicken rest briefly before serving with lemon wedges.

Rosemary Lamb Chops

 PREPARATION TIME: 10 MINUTES

 COOKING TIME: 15-20 MINUTES

SERVES: 4

Nutrition Information (Per Serving):
320 Calories / 20g Fat / 1g Carbohydrates / 28g Protein / 400mg Sodium / 0g Sugar

INGREDIENTS:

- 8 lamb chops (about 1-inch thick)
- 2 tablespoons olive oil
- 2 cloves garlic, minced
- 2 tablespoons fresh rosemary, chopped (or 1 tablespoon dried rosemary)
- Salt and pepper to taste
- Lemon wedges, for serving

DIRECTIONS:

1. Preheat the oven to 400°F (200°C).
2. In a small bowl, mix the olive oil, garlic, rosemary, salt, and pepper.
3. Rub the rosemary mixture evenly over both sides of the lamb chops.
4. Heat a large ovenproof skillet over medium-high heat. Sear the lamb chops for 2-3 minutes per side until browned.
5. Transfer the skillet to the oven and roast for 8-10 minutes for medium-rare, or longer if desired.
6. Let the lamb chops rest for a few minutes before serving with lemon wedges.

TIP: Pair this dish with a light salad or grilled asparagus with lemon.

Keftedes (Greek Meatballs)

PREPARATION TIME: 15 MINUTES

COOKING TIME: 20 MINUTES

SERVES: 4-6

Nutrition Information (Per Serving):
250 Calories / 14g Fat / 8g Carbohydrates / 22g Protein / 400mg Sodium / 2g Sugar

INGREDIENTS:

- 1 lb ground beef or a mix of beef and lamb
- 1 small onion, finely chopped
- 2 cloves garlic, minced
- 1/4 cup fresh parsley, chopped
- 1/4 cup fresh mint, chopped (optional)
- 1/4 cup breadcrumbs
- 1 egg, beaten
- 1 teaspoon dried oregano
- 1 teaspoon ground cumin
- Salt and pepper to taste
- 2 tablespoons olive oil (for frying)
- Lemon wedges, for serving

DIRECTIONS:

1. In a large bowl, mix together the ground meat, onion, garlic, parsley, mint (if using), breadcrumbs, egg, oregano, cumin, salt, and pepper until fully combined.
2. Roll the mixture into small meatballs, about 1 to 1.5 inches in diameter.
3. Heat olive oil in a large skillet over medium heat. Cook the meatballs in batches, turning to brown all sides, until they're cooked through, about 8-10 minutes.
4. Once cooked, transfer the meatballs to a paper towel-lined plate to drain excess oil.
5. Serve warm with lemon wedges on the side.

Lemon Garlic Turkey

PREPARATION TIME: 10 MINUTES

MARINATING TIME: 30 MINUTES (optional)

COOKING TIME: 25-30 MINUTES

SERVES: 4

Nutrition Information (Per Serving):
250 Calories / 12g Fat / 4g Carbohydrates / 30g Protein / 320mg Sodium / 1g Sugar

INGREDIENTS:

- 4 turkey breast cutlets (about 1 lb total)
- 3 tablespoons olive oil
- 3 cloves garlic, minced
- Juice and zest of 1 lemon
- 1 teaspoon dried oregano
- Salt and pepper to taste
- Fresh parsley, chopped (for garnish)

DIRECTIONS:

1. In a small bowl, mix together the olive oil, minced garlic, lemon juice, lemon zest, oregano, salt, and pepper.
2. Coat the turkey cutlets with the marinade, ensuring they are well covered. Let them marinate in the refrigerator for at least 30 minutes, or longer if time allows.
3. Heat a skillet over medium-high heat. Add the turkey cutlets and cook for 4-5 minutes per side, or until the turkey is golden brown and cooked through.
4. Garnish with fresh parsley and serve with lemon wedges.

TIP: Pair this dish with roasted vegetables or a light salad.

Beef Tagliata (Italian Sliced Steak)

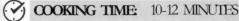 **PREPARATION TIME:** 10 MINUTES

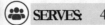 **COOKING TIME:** 10-12 MINUTES

SERVES: 4

Nutrition Information (Per Serving):
350 Calories / 22g Fat / 2g Carbohydrates / 32g Protein / 500mg Sodium / 1g Sugar

INGREDIENTS:

- 1.5 lbs ribeye or sirloin steak
- 2 tablespoons olive oil
- Salt and pepper to taste
- 1 tablespoon fresh rosemary, chopped (optional)
- 1 tablespoon fresh thyme, chopped (optional)
- 2 cups arugula
- 1/4 cup shaved Parmesan cheese
- 1 tablespoon balsamic vinegar
- Lemon wedges, for serving

DIRECTIONS:

1. Rub the steak with olive oil, and season generously with salt, pepper, rosemary, and thyme on both sides.
2. Heat a large skillet or grill pan over high heat. Once hot, add the steak and cook for 3-4 minutes per side for medium-rare, or until it reaches your desired doneness. Adjust cooking time for thicker cuts or preferred doneness. Remove the steak from the skillet and let it rest for 5 minutes.
3. While the steak is resting, arrange the arugula on a serving platter. Drizzle with a bit of olive oil and balsamic vinegar.
4. Thinly slice the steak against the grain. Place the slices over the arugula. Top with shaved Parmesan and a squeeze of lemon juice. Serve immediately with lemon wedges on the side.

Greek-Style Pork Tenderloin

PREPARATION TIME: 10 MINUTES

MARINATING TIME: 1 HOUR (optional for enhanced flavor)

COOKING TIME: 20-25 MINUTES

SERVES: 4

Nutrition Information (Per Serving):
320 Calories / 15g Fat / 2g Carbohydrates / 40g Protein / 350mg Sodium / 1g Sugar

INGREDIENTS:

- 1 lb pork tenderloin
- 3 tablespoons olive oil
- Juice and zest of 1 lemon
- 3 cloves garlic, minced
- 1 tablespoon fresh oregano, chopped (or 1 teaspoon dried oregano)
- 1 teaspoon fresh thyme, chopped (or 1/2 teaspoon dried thyme)
- Salt and pepper to taste
- Fresh parsley, chopped (for garnish)
- Lemon wedges, for serving

DIRECTIONS:

1. In a small bowl, mix olive oil, lemon juice, zest, garlic, oregano, thyme, salt, and pepper.
2. Marinate the pork in the mixture for at least 1 hour in the refrigerator.
3. Preheat the grill to medium-high heat (375°F to 400°F) or the oven to 400°F (200°C).
4. Grill or roast the pork for 20-25 minutes, turning occasionally, until the internal temperature reaches 145°F (63°C).
5. Let the pork rest for 5-10 minutes before slicing. Garnish with parsley and serve with lemon wedges.

TIP: Pair with a Greek salad or roasted potatoes for a complete Mediterranean meal.

Herb-Crusted Mediterranean Pork Chops

PREPARATION TIME: 10 MINUTES

COOKING TIME: 20-25 MINUTES

SERVES: 4

Nutrition Information (Per Serving):
400 Calories / 25g Fat / 2g Carbohydrates / 38g Protein / 450mg Sodium / 1g Sugar

INGREDIENTS:

- 4 bone-in pork chops (about 1 inch thick)
- 2 tablespoons olive oil
- 1 tablespoon fresh rosemary, chopped (or 1 teaspoon dried)
- 1 tablespoon fresh thyme, chopped (or 1 teaspoon dried)
- 1 teaspoon dried oregano
- 3 cloves garlic, minced
- Zest of 1 lemon
- Salt and pepper to taste
- Lemon wedges, for serving
- Fresh parsley, chopped (for garnish)

DIRECTIONS:

1. In a small bowl, mix together the olive oil, rosemary, thyme, oregano, minced garlic, lemon zest, salt, and pepper.
2. Rub the herb mixture evenly over both sides of the pork chops, pressing it in to adhere well.
3. Preheat your oven to 375°F (190°C). Heat a large ovenproof skillet over medium-high heat. Once hot, add the pork chops and sear for 2-3 minutes on each side until golden brown.
4. Transfer the skillet to the oven and roast for 10-15 minutes, or until the internal temperature reaches 145°F (63°C).
5. Remove the pork chops from the oven and let them rest for 5 minutes before serving. Garnish with fresh parsley and serve with lemon wedges. Add your favorite side dish or salad.

Gyros (Greek Chicken Wraps)

PREPARATION TIME: 15 MINUTES

MARINATING TIME: 1 HOUR (optional for enhanced flavor)

COOKING TIME: 10-15 MINUTES

SERVES: 4

Nutrition Information (Per Serving):
350 Calories / 12g Fat / 25g Carbohydrates / 35g Protein / 400mg Sodium / 4g Sugar

INGREDIENTS:

- 1 lb chicken breasts or thighs, cut into thin strips
- 3 tablespoons olive oil
- Juice of 1 lemon
- 3 cloves garlic, minced
- 1 teaspoon dried oregano
- 1 teaspoon ground cumin
- 1/2 teaspoon smoked paprika
- Salt and pepper to taste
- 4 pita breads
- 1 cup tzatziki sauce (see recipe on p. 22)
- 1 small red onion, thinly sliced
- 1 tomato, diced
- 1/2 cucumber, sliced
- Fresh parsley, chopped (for garnish)

DIRECTIONS:

1. In a large bowl, mix together olive oil, lemon juice, minced garlic, oregano, cumin, smoked paprika, salt, and pepper. Add the chicken strips and toss to coat evenly. Marinate in the refrigerator for at least 1 hour, or longer if time allows.
2. Heat a skillet or grill pan over medium-high heat. Add the marinated chicken strips and cook for 4-5 minutes per side, until the chicken is cooked through and slightly charred.
3. Warm the pita breads in the skillet or microwave. Spread a generous amount of tzatziki sauce over each pita. Top with cooked chicken strips, sliced red onion, diced tomato, and cucumber slices.
4. Garnish with fresh parsley and wrap the pita around the fillings. Serve immediately.

Mediterranean Beef Kabobs

PREPARATION TIME: 15 MINUTES

MARINATING TIME: 1-2 HOURS (optional for enhanced flavor)

COOKING TIME: 10-15 MINUTES

SERVES: 4

Nutrition Information (Per Serving):
350 Calories / 20g Fat / 5g Carbohydrates / 35g Protein / 450mg Sodium / 2g Sugar

INGREDIENTS:

- 1.5 lbs beef sirloin or tenderloin, cut into 1-inch cubes
- 1/4 cup olive oil
- Juice of 1 lemon
- 3 cloves garlic, minced
- 1 tablespoon dried oregano
- 1 teaspoon ground cumin
- 1 teaspoon paprika
- Salt and pepper to taste
- 1 red (or yellow, green) bell pepper, cut into 1-inch pieces
- 1 red onion, cut into 1-inch pieces
- Wooden or metal skewers
- Fresh parsley, chopped (for garnish)
- Lemon wedges, for serving

DIRECTIONS:

1. In a large mixing bowl, whisk together the olive oil, lemon juice, minced garlic, dried oregano, ground cumin, paprika, salt, and pepper. Ensure the marinade is well mixed.

2. Add the beef cubes to the marinade and toss to coat evenly. Cover the bowl with plastic wrap and refrigerate for 1-2 hours, or overnight for deeper flavor. Marinating is optional but recommended for tender and flavorful meat.

3. If using wooden skewers, soak them in water for at least 30 minutes before grilling to prevent them from burning.

4. Thread the marinated beef cubes onto the skewers, alternating with pieces of red bell pepper and red onion. Aim for an even distribution of meat and vegetables on each skewer.

5. Preheat your grill to medium-high heat (around 400°F or 200°C). Ensure the grates are clean and lightly oiled to prevent sticking.

6. Place the skewers on the grill and cook for 3-4 minutes on each side, turning occasionally. Grill until the beef is browned on the outside and cooked to your desired level of doneness. The vegetables should be tender and slightly charred.

7. Remove the kabobs from the grill and let them rest for a few minutes. Garnish with freshly chopped parsley and serve with lemon wedges on the side.

TIP: Pair these kabobs with a side of tzatziki sauce, grilled pita bread, or a Mediterranean salad for a complete meal.

Mediterranean Beef and Vegetable Stew

PREPARATION TIME: 20 MINUTES

COOKING TIME: 2 HOURS

SERVES: 4-6

Nutrition Information (Per Serving):
400 Calories / 18g Fat / 20g Carbohydrates / 35g Protein / 600mg Sodium / 6g Sugar

INGREDIENTS:

- 1.5 lbs beef stew meat, cut into 1-inch cubes
- 2 tablespoons olive oil
- 1 large onion, chopped
- 3 cloves garlic, minced
- 2 large carrots, sliced
- 2 zucchinis, sliced
- 1 red bell pepper, chopped
- 1 can (14.5 oz) diced tomatoes (or 3 fresh tomatoes, chopped)
- 2 cups beef broth
- 1/2 cup red wine (optional)
- 1 teaspoon dried oregano
- 1 teaspoon dried thyme
- 1 bay leaf
- Salt and pepper to taste
- Fresh parsley, chopped (for garnish)

DIRECTIONS:

1. Heat 2 tablespoons of olive oil in a large pot or Dutch oven over medium-high heat. Season the beef stew meat generously with salt and pepper. When the oil is hot but not smoking, add the beef cubes in a single layer. Brown the meat on all sides, turning occasionally, for about 5-7 minutes. Work in batches if necessary to avoid overcrowding the pot, as this will prevent proper browning. Once browned, remove the beef from the pot and set it aside on a plate.

2. In the same pot, reduce the heat to medium. Add the chopped onion to the pot, using a wooden spoon to scrape up any browned bits from the bottom (these bits add great flavor). Sauté the onions for 4-5 minutes until they begin to soften and turn translucent. Add the minced garlic and cook for an additional 1-2 minutes, stirring constantly to avoid burning.

3. Add the sliced carrots, zucchinis, and chopped red bell pepper to the pot. Stir the vegetables together and cook for about 5-7 minutes until they start to soften. The vegetables should begin to take on some color but should not be fully cooked at this stage.

4. Return the browned beef to the pot with the vegetables. Add the diced tomatoes (including their juices), beef broth, red wine (if using), dried oregano, dried thyme, and bay leaf. Stir everything together to combine. The liquid should just cover the beef and vegetables; if needed, add a bit more broth or water.

5. Increase the heat to bring the stew to a gentle boil. Once boiling, reduce the heat to low, cover the pot, and let the stew simmer for 1.5 to 2 hours. Stir occasionally to ensure the stew isn't sticking to the bottom of the pot. The beef should become tender, and the flavors should meld together nicely.

6. After the stew has simmered and the beef is tender, remove the bay leaf. Taste the stew and adjust seasoning with additional salt and pepper if needed. If the stew is too thick, you can thin it with a little more broth or water. Serve the stew hot, garnished with fresh chopped parsley.

TIP: This stew is even better the next day as the flavors continue to develop. Serve it with crusty bread, couscous, or over mashed potatoes for a hearty meal.

Domates Dolmasi (Turkish Stuffed Tomatoes)

 PREPARATION TIME: 15 MINUTES

 COOKING TIME: 45 MINUTES

 SERVES: 4

Nutrition Information (Per Serving):
220 Calories / 12g Fat / 18g Carbohydrates / 10g Protein / 280mg Sodium / 6g Sugar

INGREDIENTS:

- 4 large tomatoes
- 1/4 pound ground beef or lamb
- 1/4 cup uncooked rice
- 1/2 medium onion, finely chopped
- 1 clove garlic, minced
- 2 tablespoons fresh parsley, chopped
- 2 tablespoons fresh mint, chopped
- 1/2 teaspoon ground cumin
- 1/2 teaspoon paprika
- Salt and pepper to taste
- 1 tablespoon olive oil
- 1/2 cup water or vegetable broth
- 1 tablespoon tomato paste
- 1/2 cup yogurt (optional)

DIRECTIONS:

1. Cut off the tops of the tomatoes and scoop out the insides, leaving a thick shell. Chop and set aside the tomato pulp.
2. In a bowl, mix ground beef or lamb, rice, onion, garlic, parsley, mint, cumin, paprika, salt, pepper, and half the tomato pulp.
3. Stuff the tomatoes with the meat mixture, place them in a baking dish, and replace the tops.
4. Mix the remaining tomato pulp with olive oil, water or broth, and tomato paste. Pour around the tomatoes.
5. Cover with foil and bake at 350°F (175°C) for 45 minutes, until the tomatoes are tender.
6. Let cool slightly before serving. Garnish with fresh herbs and yogurt if desired.

Turkish Beans with Sausages

 PREPARATION TIME: 10 MINUTES

 COOKING TIME: 40 MINUTES

 SERVES: 4-6

Nutrition Information (Per Serving):
350 Calories / 18g Fat / 30g Carbohydrates / 16g Protein / 600mg Sodium / 5g Sugar

INGREDIENTS:

- 1 lb Turkish sausage (Sucuk) or another spicy sausage, sliced
- 2 tablespoons olive oil
- 1 large onion, chopped
- 3 cloves garlic, minced
- 1 can (14.5 oz) diced tomatoes
- 1 can (15 oz) white beans or cannellini beans, drained and rinsed
- 1 teaspoon ground cumin
- 1 teaspoon paprika
- 1/2 teaspoon ground black pepper, salt to taste
- 1 cup water or chicken broth
- Fresh parsley, chopped (for garnish)

DIRECTIONS:

1. Heat olive oil in a large pot over medium heat. Add the sliced sausage and cook for about 5 minutes until browned. Remove the sausage and set aside.
2. In the same pot, add the chopped onion and sauté until softened, about 5 minutes. Add the minced garlic and cook for another minute.
3. Stir in the diced tomatoes, beans, cumin, paprika, black pepper, and salt. Add the water or chicken broth, and bring the mixture to a simmer.
4. Return the sausage to the pot. Cover and cook on low heat for 30 minutes, stirring occasionally, until the flavors meld and the beans are tender.
5. Serve hot, garnished with fresh parsley.

Hanneth Lamb Shanks

 PREPARATION TIME: 20 MINUTES

 COOKING TIME: 2 HOURS 30 MINUTES

 SERVES: 4

Nutrition Information (Per Serving):
500 Calories / 28g Fat / 10g Carbohydrates / 45g Protein / 600mg Sodium / 2g Sugar

INGREDIENTS:
- 4 lamb shanks
- 3 tablespoons olive oil
- 2 large onions, sliced
- 5 cloves garlic, minced
- 2 teaspoons ground cumin
- 2 teaspoons ground coriander
- 1 teaspoon ground cinnamon
- 1 teaspoon ground turmeric
- 1 teaspoon ground black pepper
- 1 cup meat broth
- 1 cup water
- 1 can (14.5 oz) diced tomatoes
- 2 bay leaves, salt to taste
- Fresh cilantro or parsley, chopped (for garnish)

DIRECTIONS:
1. Preheat the oven to 325°F (160°C).
2. Heat olive oil in a large ovenproof pot over medium heat. Sear the lamb shanks until browned on all sides, about 8-10 minutes. Remove and set aside.
3. In the same pot, cook sliced onions until softened, about 5 minutes. Add garlic, cumin, coriander, cinnamon, turmeric, and black pepper. Stir and cook for 2 minutes.
4. Return lamb shanks to the pot. Add broth, water, diced tomatoes, and bay leaves. Bring to a simmer.
5. Cover and transfer to the oven. Cook for 2-2.5 hours, until the lamb is tender and falls off the bone.
6. Let the lamb rest for a few minutes. Garnish with fresh cilantro or parsley. Serve with couscous, rice, or mashed potatoes to soak up the rich sauce.

Spiced Chicken Wings

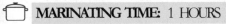 **PREPARATION TIME:** 10 MINUTES

MARINATING TIME: 1 HOURS (optional)

 **COOKING TIME:** 30-35 MINUTES

SERVES: 4

Nutrition Information (Per Serving):
320 Calories / 22g Fat / 3g Carbohydrates / 25g Protein / 450mg Sodium / 1g Sugar

INGREDIENTS:
- 2 lbs chicken wings
- 3 tablespoons olive oil
- Juice of 1 lemon
- 3 cloves garlic, minced
- 1 teaspoon ground cumin
- 1 teaspoon smoked paprika
- 1 teaspoon dried oregano
- 1/2 teaspoon ground coriander
- 1/2 teaspoon ground cinnamon
- Salt and pepper to taste
- Fresh parsley, chopped (for garnish)

DIRECTIONS:
1. In a large bowl, mix olive oil, lemon juice, garlic, cumin, paprika, oregano, coriander, cinnamon, salt, and pepper. Add chicken wings and toss to coat. Marinate for 1 hour if time allows.
2. Preheat oven to 400°F (200°C). Line a baking sheet with parchment paper.
3. Arrange the wings in a single layer on the baking sheet. Bake for 30-35 minutes, turning halfway through, until the wings are golden and crispy.
4. Garnish with fresh parsley and serve hot.

TIP: Pair with a side of tzatziki or hummus for dipping.

Lahmacun (Turkish Style Flatbread)

⚔ **PREPARATION TIME:** 20 MINUTES

🥣 **DOUGH RISING TIME:** 30 MINUTES

⏱ **COOKING TIME:** 10-12 MINUTES

👥 **SERVES:** (makes 8 small flatbreads)
4-6

Nutrition Information (Per Serving): 300 Calories / 12g Fat / 32g Carbohydrates / 14g Protein / 450mg Sodium / 2g Sugar

INGREDIENTS:

For the dough:
- 2 cups all-purpose flour
- 1 teaspoon salt
- 1 teaspoon sugar
- 1 teaspoon active dry yeast
- 3/4 cup warm water
- 2 tablespoons olive oil

For the topping:
- 1/2 lb ground lamb or beef
- 1 onion, finely chopped
- 2 cloves garlic, minced
- 1 tomato, finely chopped
- 1 tablespoon tomato paste
- 1/2 teaspoon ground cumin
- 1/2 teaspoon ground paprika
- 1/4 teaspoon ground cinnamon (optional)
- 1/4 teaspoon red pepper flakes (optional)
- Salt and pepper to taste
- Fresh parsley, chopped (for garnish)
- Lemon wedges (for serving)

DIRECTIONS:

1. Prepare the dough: In a large bowl, mix flour, salt, sugar, and yeast. Gradually add warm water and olive oil, mixing until a soft dough forms. Knead for about 5 minutes until smooth and elastic. Cover the dough and let it rest for 30 minutes.

2. Prepare the topping: In a mixing bowl, combine the ground meat, chopped onion, garlic, tomato, tomato paste, cumin, paprika, cinnamon (if using), red pepper flakes, salt, and pepper. Mix well until all ingredients are evenly combined.

3. Assemble the Lahmacun: Preheat your oven to 450°F (230°C). Divide the dough into 8 equal portions. Roll out each portion on a floured surface into thin circles, about 8 inches in diameter. Spread a thin layer of the meat mixture over each circle.

4. Bake: Place the topped flatbreads on a baking sheet and bake for 10-12 minutes, or until the edges are crispy and the meat is cooked through.

5. Serve: Garnish with fresh parsley and serve with lemon wedges. Lahmacun is traditionally rolled up and eaten like a wrap.

TIP: You can serve Lahmacun with a side of fresh salad or yogurt for a complete meal.

Lemon and Caper Chicken Piccata

PREPARATION TIME: 10 MINUTES

COOKING TIME: 15-20 MINUTES

SERVES: 4

Nutrition Information (Per Serving):
320 Calories / 18g Fat / 6g Carbohydrates / 28g Protein / 500mg Sodium / 1g Sugar

INGREDIENTS:

- 4 boneless, skinless chicken breasts
- 1/4 cup flour (for dredging)
- Salt and pepper to taste
- 3 tablespoons olive oil
- 3 cloves garlic, minced
- 1/2 cup chicken broth
- Juice of 1 lemon
- 2 tablespoons capers, drained
- 2 tablespoons unsalted butter
- Fresh parsley, chopped (for garnish)
- Lemon slices, for serving

DIRECTIONS:

1. Season the chicken breasts with salt and pepper, then dredge them in flour, shaking off any excess.
2. Heat the olive oil in a large skillet over medium-high heat. Cook the chicken for 3-4 minutes on each side until golden and cooked through. Remove the chicken from the skillet and set it aside.
3. In the same skillet, add the minced garlic and cook for about 1 minute until fragrant. Pour in the chicken broth and lemon juice, scraping up any browned bits from the bottom of the skillet. Let it simmer for 2-3 minutes.
4. Stir in the capers and butter, cooking until the butter melts and the sauce is smooth.
5. Return the chicken to the skillet, spooning the sauce over the top. Cook for an additional 3-5 minutes or until the chicken is fully cooked through.
6. Garnish with fresh parsley and serve with your favorite side dish.

Kofta Kebab

PREPARATION TIME: 15 MINUTES

COOKING TIME: 10 MINUTES

SERVES: 4

Nutrition Information (Per Serving):
400 Calories / 24g Fat / 3g Carbohydrates / 28g Protein / 500mg Sodium / 1g Sugar

INGREDIENTS:

- 1 ½ lb ground beef
- 1 small onion, finely grated
- 2 garlic cloves, minced
- 1 ½ cups fresh parsley, chopped
- 2 teaspoons dried oregano
- Salt and pepper, to taste
- 1 egg (optional, for binding)
- 2 tablespoons olive oil (for brushing)

DIRECTIONS:

1. In a large bowl, combine the ground beef, grated onion, minced garlic, chopped parsley, dried oregano, and the egg (if using). Season with a big pinch of salt and pepper. Mix well until all ingredients are evenly combined.
2. Divide the mixture into 8 equal parts. Shape each portion into a cylinder around a metal skewer, pressing firmly to ensure the mixture adheres.
3. Heat 3 tablespoons of olive oil in a griddle pan over medium heat. Once hot, add the kofta kebabs.
4. Cook the kebabs for 8-10 minutes, turning every 1-2 minutes until they are deeply golden and lightly charred on all sides.
5. Serve the kofta kebabs hot, alongside tzatziki and a fresh Greek salad.

Lahanodolmades (Stuffed Cabbage Rolls)

⚔ **PREPARATION TIME:** 30 MINUTES

🕐 **COOKING TIME:** 1 HOUR

👥 **SERVES:** 4-6

Nutrition Information (Per Serving):
350 Calories / 15g Fat / 25g Carbohydrates / 25g Protein / 600mg Sodium / 4g Sugar

INGREDIENTS:

- 1 large head of cabbage
- 1 lb ground beef or lamb
- 1/2 cup uncooked rice
- 1 large onion, finely chopped
- 3 cloves garlic, minced
- 2 tablespoons olive oil
- 1/4 cup fresh parsley, chopped
- 1/4 cup fresh dill, chopped
- 1 teaspoon dried oregano
- Salt and pepper to taste
- 1/4 cup lemon juice
- 2 cups chicken or vegetable broth
- 2 eggs (optional, for avgolemono sauce)

DIRECTIONS:

1. Prepare the cabbage: Bring a large pot of salted water to a boil. Carefully remove the cabbage leaves from the head and blanch them in the boiling water for 2-3 minutes until softened. Remove the leaves and let them cool.

2. Prepare the filling: In a large bowl, mix the ground beef or lamb, uncooked rice, chopped onion, garlic, olive oil, parsley, dill, oregano, salt, and pepper until well combined.

3. Stuff the cabbage leaves: Place a spoonful of the filling onto each cabbage leaf. Fold the sides over the filling and roll it up tightly, starting from the stem end.

4. Arrange and cook: Place the cabbage rolls seam-side down in a large pot. Pour the lemon juice and broth over the rolls. Cover the pot and simmer on low heat for about 1 hour, or until the meat is cooked through and the rice is tender.

5. Optional - Avgolemono Sauce: Whisk the eggs with some of the hot cooking liquid from the pot until frothy. Gradually add the lemon juice while continuing to whisk. Pour the sauce over the cabbage rolls and cook for an additional 5 minutes, until the sauce thickens slightly.

6. Serve: Garnish with additional fresh herbs and serve hot.

TIP: Serve with a side of Greek yogurt or a simple cucumber salad to complement the rich flavors of the cabbage rolls.

Lamb Moussaka (Greek Layered Eggplant)

PREPARATION TIME: 30 MINUTES

COOKING TIME: 1 HOUR 30 MINUTES

SERVES: 4

Nutrition Information (Per Serving):
500 Calories / 30g Fat / 25g Carbohydrates / 35g Protein / 600mg Sodium / 5g Sugar

INGREDIENTS:

For the meat sauce:
- 3/4 lb ground lamb
- 1 medium onion, finely chopped
- 2 cloves garlic, minced
- 1 can (8 oz) diced tomatoes
- 1 tablespoon tomato paste
- 1/4 cup red wine (optional)
- 1/2 teaspoon ground cinnamon
- 1/4 teaspoon ground allspice
- 1/2 teaspoon dried oregano
- Salt and pepper to taste

For the eggplant layers:
- 1-1/2 large eggplants, sliced into 1/4-inch rounds
- Olive oil, for brushing
- Salt

For the béchamel sauce:
- 3 tablespoons butter
- 3 tablespoons all-purpose flour
- 1-1/2 cups milk, warmed
- 1/4 teaspoon ground nutmeg
- 1/3 cup grated Parmesan cheese
- 1 egg, beaten

DIRECTIONS:

1. Prepare the eggplant: Preheat the oven to 400°F (200°C). Arrange the eggplant slices on a baking sheet, brush with olive oil, and sprinkle with salt. Roast for 20-25 minutes until soft and golden, turning once. Set aside.

2. Cook the meat sauce: In a large skillet, heat olive oil over medium heat. Add the chopped onion and garlic, sautéing until softened. Add the ground lamb and cook until browned. Stir in the diced tomatoes, tomato paste, red wine (if using), cinnamon, allspice, oregano, salt, and pepper. Simmer for 20-25 minutes until the sauce thickens.

3. Prepare the béchamel sauce: In a saucepan, melt the butter over medium heat. Stir in the flour and cook for 1-2 minutes until smooth. Gradually add the warmed milk, whisking constantly until the sauce thickens. Remove from heat and stir in nutmeg, cheese, and beaten egg.

4. Assemble the moussaka: In a medium-sized baking dish, layer half of the roasted eggplant slices on the bottom. Spread the meat sauce evenly over the eggplant. Top with the remaining eggplant slices. Pour the béchamel sauce over the top, spreading it evenly.

5. Bake: Reduce the oven temperature to 350°F (175°C). Bake the moussaka for 45-50 minutes until the top is golden and bubbling. Let it rest for 10-15 minutes before serving.

6. Serve: Slice the moussaka and serve warm, garnished with fresh herbs if desired.

TIP: Serve with a side of Greek salad or crusty bread to soak up the delicious sauce.

Chapter **7**

DESSERTS

Lemon Olive Oil Cake

 PREPARATION TIME: 15 MINUTES

 COOKING TIME: 45 MINUTES

SERVES: 8-10

Nutrition Information (Per Serving):
280 Calories / 14g Fat / 34g Carbohydrates / 4g Protein / 200mg Sodium / 18g Sugar

INGREDIENTS:

- 1 1/2 cups all-purpose flour
- 1 cup granulated sugar
- 1/2 teaspoon baking soda
- 1/2 teaspoon baking powder
- 1/4 teaspoon salt
- 1/2 cup extra-virgin olive oil
- 1/2 cup whole milk or almond milk
- 3 large eggs
- Zest of 2 lemons
- 1/4 cup freshly squeezed lemon juice
- 1 teaspoon vanilla extract

DIRECTIONS:

1. Preheat the oven to 350°F (175°C). Grease a 9-inch round cake pan and line the bottom with parchment paper.
2. In a large mixing bowl, whisk together the flour, sugar, baking soda, baking powder, and salt.
3. In a separate bowl, whisk together the olive oil, milk, eggs, lemon zest, lemon juice, and vanilla extract until smooth.
4. Gradually add the wet ingredients to the dry ingredients, stirring just until combined. Be careful not to overmix.
5. Pour the batter into the prepared cake pan and smooth the top. Bake for 40-45 minutes, or until a toothpick inserted into the center comes out clean.
6. Allow the cake to cool in the pan for 10 minutes, then turn it out onto a wire rack to cool completely. Dust with powdered sugar before serving if desired.

Honey Ricotta with Fresh Berries

 PREPARATION TIME: 10 MINUTES

 COOKING TIME: 10 MINUTES

 SERVES: 4

Nutrition Information (Per Serving):
220 Calories / 12g Fat / 19g Carbohydrates / 8g Protein / 80mg Sodium / 16g Sugar

INGREDIENTS:

- 1 cup ricotta cheese
- 2 tablespoons honey
- 1 teaspoon vanilla extract
- 1 cup mixed fresh berries (strawberries, blueberries, raspberries)
- 1/4 cup sliced almonds or chopped nuts (optional)
- Fresh mint leaves for garnish (optional)

DIRECTIONS:

1. In a medium bowl, mix the ricotta cheese, honey, and vanilla extract until smooth and creamy.
2. Divide the ricotta mixture among four serving dishes.
3. Top each dish with a generous portion of fresh berries.
4. Sprinkle with sliced almonds or chopped nuts if desired.
5. Garnish with fresh mint leaves for an extra touch of color and flavor.
6. Serve immediately.

TIP: For an added layer of flavor, drizzle a little more honey over the berries just before serving.

Traditional Baklava

 PREPARATION TIME: 30 MINUTES

 COOKING TIME: 45-50 MINUTES

SERVES: 24-30 PIECES

Nutrition Information (Per Piece):
290 Calories / 19g Fat / 28g Carbohydrates / 3g Protein / 95mg Sodium / 18g Sugar

INGREDIENTS:

For the Baklava:

- 1 package (16 oz) phyllo dough, thawed
- 2 cups walnuts, finely chopped
- 2 cups pistachios, finely chopped
- 1 teaspoon ground cinnamon
- 1/2 teaspoon ground cloves (optional)
- 1 cup unsalted butter, melted

For the Syrup:

- 1 cup water
- 1 cup granulated sugar
- 1/2 cup honey
- 1 tablespoon lemon juice
- 1 cinnamon stick
- 1 teaspoon vanilla extract

DIRECTIONS:

1. Preheat the oven to 350°F (175°C). Grease a 9x13-inch baking dish with melted butter.

2. Prepare the nut filling: In a bowl, mix together the chopped walnuts, pistachios, ground cinnamon, and ground cloves (if using).

3. Assemble the baklava: Lay one sheet of phyllo dough in the bottom of the prepared baking dish and brush with melted butter. Repeat with 7 more sheets, brushing each one with butter. Sprinkle about 1/4 of the nut mixture evenly over the phyllo. Continue layering 8 more sheets of phyllo, buttering each sheet, then add another layer of nuts. Repeat the process until all the nuts are used, ending with 8 layers of buttered phyllo sheets on top.

4. Cut the baklava: Using a sharp knife, cut the baklava into diamond or square shapes before baking.

5. Bake the baklava: Place the baking dish in the preheated oven and bake for 45-50 minutes, or until the baklava is golden brown and crisp.

6. Prepare the syrup: While the baklava is baking, combine the water, sugar, honey, lemon juice, and cinnamon stick in a saucepan. Bring to a boil, then reduce the heat and simmer for 10 minutes. Remove from heat and stir in the vanilla extract. Let the syrup cool slightly.

7. Add the syrup: As soon as the baklava comes out of the oven, remove the cinnamon stick from the syrup and pour the syrup evenly over the hot baklava. Make sure the syrup covers all pieces.

8. Cool and serve: Allow the baklava to cool completely, letting the syrup soak in for at least 4 hours or overnight. Serve at room temperature.

TIP: Baklava can be stored at room temperature for several days, covered lightly with foil. The flavors improve as it sits, making it an ideal make-ahead dessert.

Orange and Almond Cake

 PREPARATION TIME: 20 MINUTES

 COOKING TIME: 2 HOURS

 SERVES: 8-10

Nutrition Information (Per Serving):
300 Calories / 16g Fat / 32g Carbohydrates / 7g Protein / 150mg Sodium / 22g Sugar

INGREDIENTS:

- 2 large oranges
- 1 1/2 cups almond flour (finely ground almonds)
- 1 cup granulated sugar
- 6 large eggs
- 1 teaspoon baking powder
- 1/4 teaspoon salt
- Zest of 1 orange
- 1 teaspoon vanilla extract
- Powdered sugar for dusting (optional)

DIRECTIONS:

1. Place oranges in a pot, cover with water, and boil. Simmer for 1 hour until soft, then cool.
2. Preheat the oven to 350°F (175°C). Grease and line a 9-inch round cake pan.
3. Quarter the cooled oranges, remove seeds, and puree them in a food processor.
4. In a bowl, mix almond flour, sugar, baking powder, and salt. In another bowl, beat the eggs, then add the orange puree, zest, and vanilla. Combine wet and dry ingredients.
5. Pour the batter into the pan and bake for 50-60 minutes until a toothpick comes out clean. Cover with foil if browning too quickly.
6. Cool the cake for 10 minutes in the pan, then transfer to a wire rack to cool completely. Dust with powdered sugar if desired.

Stuffed Dates with Nuts and Goat Cheese

 **PREPARATION TIME:** 15 MINUTES

COOKING TIME: 15 MINUTES

SERVES: 8-10

Nutrition Information (Per Serving):
120 Calories / 6g Fat / 14g Carbohydrates / 3g Protein / 60mg Sodium / 11g Sugar

INGREDIENTS:

- 20 Medjool dates, pitted
- 4 oz goat cheese, softened
- 1/4 cup chopped nuts (such as almonds, walnuts, or pistachios)
- 1 tablespoon honey (optional, for drizzling)
- Fresh herbs (such as thyme or rosemary) for garnish (optional)

DIRECTIONS:

1. Slice each date lengthwise to create an opening, being careful not to cut all the way through.
2. Fill each date with about 1/2 teaspoon of goat cheese.
3. Sprinkle the stuffed dates with chopped nuts.
4. Arrange the dates on a serving platter.
5. If desired, drizzle with honey and garnish with fresh herbs.
6. Serve immediately.

TIP: For added flavor, lightly toast the nuts before using them to fill the dates.

Honey Almond Cookies

 PREPARATION TIME: 15 MINUTES

 COOKING TIME: 12-15 MINUTES

 SERVES: 20 COOKIES

Nutrition Information (Per Cookie):
120 Calories / 7g Fat / 12g Carbohydrates / 2g Protein / 50mg Sodium / 8g Sugar

INGREDIENTS:

- 1 1/2 cups almond flour
- 1/4 cup honey
- 1/4 cup unsalted butter, melted
- 1/2 teaspoon vanilla extract
- 1/4 teaspoon almond extract (optional)
- 1/4 teaspoon baking powder
- 1/4 teaspoon salt
- 1/4 cup sliced almonds, for topping

DIRECTIONS:

1. Preheat the oven to 350°F (175°C) and line a baking sheet with parchment paper.
2. In a bowl, mix almond flour, baking powder, and salt. In another bowl, whisk melted butter, honey, vanilla, and almond extract.
3. Combine wet and dry ingredients to form a dough.
4. Roll tablespoon-sized portions of dough into balls, flatten slightly, and place on the baking sheet. Top with sliced almonds.
5. Bake for 12-15 minutes until the edges are golden. Cool on the baking sheet for a few minutes, then transfer to a wire rack to cool completely.

Fig and Honey Tart

 PREPARATION TIME: 20 MINUTES

 COOKING TIME: 25-30 MINUTES

SERVES: 8-10

Nutrition Information (Per Serving):
260 Calories / 14g Fat / 30g Carbohydrates / 4g Protein / 120mg Sodium / 15g Sugar

INGREDIENTS:

- 1 sheet of puff pastry, thawed
- 8-10 fresh figs, sliced
- 1/2 cup ricotta cheese
- 2 tablespoons honey (plus more for drizzling)
- 1 teaspoon vanilla extract
- 1/4 teaspoon ground cinnamon
- 1/4 cup chopped walnuts or pistachios
- Fresh thyme or mint leaves for garnish (optional)

DIRECTIONS:

1. Preheat the oven to 375°F (190°C). Line a baking sheet with parchment paper.
2. Roll out the puff pastry sheet onto the prepared baking sheet.
3. In a bowl, mix ricotta, honey, vanilla, and cinnamon. Spread the mixture evenly over the puff pastry, leaving a 1-inch border.
4. Arrange the fig slices on top of the ricotta mixture. Sprinkle with chopped nuts.
5. Fold the edges of the puff pastry over the filling to create a border.
6. Bake for 25-30 minutes, or until the pastry is golden and crisp.
7. Drizzle with extra honey and garnish with fresh thyme or mint leaves if desired. Serve warm or at room temperature.

Yogurt and Berry Parfait

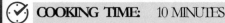 **PREPARATION TIME:** 10 MINUTES

COOKING TIME: 10 MINUTES

SERVES: 4

Nutrition Information (Per Serving):
180 Calories / 6g Fat / 25g Carbohydrates / 7g Protein /
70mg Sodium / 18g Sugar

INGREDIENTS:

- 2 cups Greek yogurt
- 2 tablespoons honey or maple syrup
- 1 teaspoon vanilla extract
- 2 cups mixed berries (strawberries, blueberries, raspberries)
- 1/2 cup granola
- Fresh mint leaves for garnish (optional)

DIRECTIONS:

1. In a medium bowl, stir together the Greek yogurt, honey, and vanilla extract until smooth and well combined. Taste and adjust the sweetness by adding more honey if desired.
2. Spoon a layer of the yogurt mixture into the bottom of each serving glass or bowl.
3. Top the yogurt with a layer of mixed berries, followed by a sprinkle of granola.
4. Add another layer of yogurt, then more berries and granola.
5. Continue layering until the glasses are full, finishing with berries and a sprinkle of granola on top.
6. Garnish each parfait with fresh mint leaves if desired.

Panna Cotta with Honey

PREPARATION TIME: 10 MINUTES

COOKING TIME: 10 MINUTES

CHILLING TIME: 4 HOURS

SERVES: 6

Nutrition Information (Per Serving):
250 Calories / 15g Fat / 22g Carbohydrates / 5g Protein /
35mg Sodium / 18g Sugar

INGREDIENTS:

- 2 cups heavy cream
- 1 cup whole milk
- 1/3 cup honey (plus more for drizzling)
- 1 teaspoon vanilla extract
- 2 1/2 teaspoons unflavored gelatin
- 3 tablespoons cold water
- Fresh berries or chopped nuts for garnish (optional)

DIRECTIONS:

1. In a small bowl, sprinkle the gelatin over the cold water and let it sit for 5 minutes to bloom.
2. In a saucepan, combine the heavy cream, whole milk, and honey. Heat the mixture over medium heat, stirring occasionally, until it's just about to boil. Remove from heat.
3. Stir in the bloomed gelatin and vanilla extract until fully dissolved.
4. Divide the mixture evenly among 6 ramekins or serving glasses.
5. Allow the panna cotta to cool to room temperature, then cover and refrigerate for at least 4 hours, or until set.
6. To serve, drizzle with additional honey and garnish with fresh berries or chopped nuts if desired.

Honey and Cinnamon Baked Grapefruit

 PREPARATION TIME: 5 MINUTES

 COOKING TIME: 10 -12 MINUTES

SERVES: 4

Nutrition Information (Per Serving):
90 Calories / 2g Fat / 20g Carbohydrates / 1g Protein / 0mg Sodium / 18g Sugar

INGREDIENTS:

- 2 large grapefruits
- 4 tablespoons honey
- 1 teaspoon ground cinnamon
- 1/2 teaspoon vanilla extract (optional)
- Fresh mint leaves for garnish (optional)

DIRECTIONS:

1. Preheat the oven to 375°F (190°C). Line a baking sheet with parchment paper.
2. Cut the grapefruits in half and use a small knife to loosen the segments for easier eating.
3. Place the grapefruit halves on the prepared baking sheet.
4. Drizzle each grapefruit half with 1 tablespoon of honey and sprinkle with ground cinnamon. Add a few drops of vanilla extract if using.
5. Bake in the preheated oven for 10 - 12 minutes, or until the tops are slightly caramelized.
6. Remove from the oven and let cool for a few minutes. Garnish with fresh mint leaves if desired and serve warm.

Pomegranate and Nuts Frozen Yogurt Slice

PREPARATION TIME: 15 MINUTES

COOKING TIME: NIONE

FREEZING TIME: 4 HOURS

SERVES: 8-10

Nutrition Information (Per Serving):
180 Calories / 8g Fat / 22g Carbohydrates / 6g Protein / 40mg Sodium / 15g Sugar

INGREDIENTS:

- 2 cups Greek yogurt (plain or vanilla)
- 1/4 cup honey or maple syrup
- 1 teaspoon vanilla extract
- 1/2 cup pomegranate seeds
- 1/2 cup mixed nuts (such as almonds, walnuts, or pistachios), chopped
- 1/4 cup dried cranberries or raisins (optional)

DIRECTIONS:

1. Line a loaf pan with parchment paper, leaving some overhang on the sides for easy removal.
2. In a mixing bowl, stir together the Greek yogurt, honey or maple syrup, and vanilla extract until well combined.
3. Fold in the pomegranate seeds, chopped nuts, and dried cranberries or raisins (if using).
4. Pour the mixture into the prepared loaf pan, spreading it evenly with a spatula.
5. Cover the pan with plastic wrap and freeze for at least 4 hours, or until firm.
6. Once frozen, use the parchment overhang to lift the yogurt slice out of the pan. Cut into slices or bars.
7. Serve immediately or store in an airtight container in the freezer for up to 2 weeks.

Grapes in Muscat Syrup

PREPARATION TIME: 5 MINUTES

COOKING TIME: NONE

CHILLING TIME: 1 HOUR

SERVES: 4

Nutrition Information (Per Serving):
120 Calories / 0g Fat / 28g Carbohydrates / 1g Protein / 0mg Sodium / 26g Sugar

INGREDIENTS:

- 2 cups seedless grapes (red or green)
- 1/2 cup Muscat wine (or any sweet dessert wine)
- 2 tablespoons honey
- 1 teaspoon lemon juice
- 1/2 teaspoon vanilla extract
- Fresh mint leaves for garnish (optional)

DIRECTIONS:

1. In a small saucepan, combine the Muscat wine, honey, lemon juice, and vanilla extract.
2. Bring the mixture to a gentle simmer over low heat, stirring until the honey is fully dissolved.
3. Remove from heat and let the syrup cool to room temperature.
4. Place the grapes in a serving bowl or divide them into individual dessert glasses.
5. Pour the cooled syrup over the grapes, making sure they are well coated.
6. Cover and refrigerate for at least 1 hour to allow the flavors to meld.
7. Serve the chilled grapes in their syrup, garnished with fresh mint leaves if desired.

Mahalabia (Middle Eastern Milk Pudding)

PREPARATION TIME: 10 MINUTES

COOKING TIME: 10 MINUTES

CHILLING TIME: 1-2 HOURS

SERVES: 6

Nutrition Information (Per Serving):
180 Calories / 6g Fat / 25g Carbohydrates / 6g Protein / 50mg Sodium / 20g Sugar

INGREDIENTS:

- 4 cups whole milk
- 1/2 cup granulated sugar
- 1/4 cup cornstarch
- 1 tablespoon rose water or orange blossom water (or substitute with 1 teaspoon vanilla extract)
- 1/4 cup chopped pistachios or almonds, for garnish
- Pomegranate seeds for garnish (optional)

DIRECTIONS:

1. In a small bowl, dissolve the cornstarch in 1/2 cup of the milk, stirring until smooth.
2. In a medium saucepan, combine the remaining milk and sugar. Heat over medium heat, stirring until the sugar dissolves.
3. Gradually add the cornstarch mixture to the saucepan, whisking constantly to avoid lumps. Continue to cook, stirring constantly, until the mixture thickens and coats the back of a spoon, about 10 minutes.
4. Remove from heat and stir in the rose water, orange blossom water, or vanilla extract.
5. Pour the Mahalabia into individual serving dishes or bowls. Let it cool to room temperature, then refrigerate for 2-3 hours, or until set.
6. Garnish with chopped pistachios or almonds and pomegranate seeds if desired, before serving.

Tiramisu

✕ **PREPARATION TIME:**	5 MINUTES	
⏱ **COOKING TIME:**	25 MINUTE	
❄ **CHILLING TIME:**	4 HOURS	(or overnight)
👥 **SERVES:**	8-10	

Nutrition Information (Per Serving):
300 Calories / 18g Fat / 32g Carbohydrates / 5g Protein / 120mg Sodium / 20g Sugar

INGREDIENTS:

- 1 cup strong brewed coffee, cooled
- 2 tablespoons coffee liqueur (optional)
- 3 large eggs, separated
- 1/2 cup granulated sugar, divided
- 1 cup mascarpone cheese, softened
- 1 teaspoon vanilla extract
- 24-30 ladyfinger cookies (savoiardi)
- 2 tablespoons unsweetened cocoa powder
- Chocolate shavings or cocoa powder for garnish (optional)

DIRECTIONS:

1. Prepare the coffee mixture: In a shallow dish, combine the cooled brewed coffee and coffee liqueur (if using). Set this mixture aside for dipping the ladyfingers later.

2. Make the mascarpone filling: In a mixing bowl, beat the egg yolks and 1/4 cup of sugar together using an electric mixer on medium speed. Continue beating until the mixture becomes thick, pale, and creamy, about 3-5 minutes. Add the softened mascarpone cheese and vanilla extract, and mix on low speed until smooth and well combined.

3. Whip the egg whites: In a separate clean bowl, whisk the egg whites with the remaining 1/4 cup of sugar using an electric mixer. Beat until stiff peaks form, meaning the egg whites hold their shape when the whisk is lifted. This will give the tiramisu a light, airy texture.

4. Combine the mixtures: Gently fold the whipped egg whites into the mascarpone mixture in three additions. Use a spatula and fold carefully to keep the mixture light and fluffy. This ensures a smooth and airy filling.

5. Assemble the tiramisu: Quickly dip each ladyfinger into the coffee mixture for about 1-2 seconds, ensuring they absorb the coffee but do not become soggy. Arrange a single layer of dipped ladyfingers in the bottom of an 8x8-inch dish or similarly sized serving dish. Spread half of the mascarpone mixture evenly over the ladyfingers. Repeat the process with a second layer of dipped ladyfingers and the remaining mascarpone mixture.

6. Finish and chill: Sift the unsweetened cocoa powder evenly over the top layer of mascarpone. Cover the dish with plastic wrap and refrigerate for at least 4 hours, or preferably overnight. This chilling time allows the flavors to meld and the tiramisu to set properly.

7. Serve: Before serving, optionally garnish with chocolate shavings or an additional dusting of cocoa powder. Slice the tiramisu into squares and serve chilled.

TIP: For a non-alcoholic version, omit the coffee liqueur and use additional brewed coffee.

Revani
(Semolina Cake)

PREPARATION TIME: 15 MINUTES

COOKING TIME: 30 MINUTES

RESTING TIME: 2 HOURS   (for soaking)

SERVES: 6-8

Nutrition Information (Per Serving): 360 Calories / 12g Fat / 58g Carbohydrates / 6g Protein / 50mg Sodium / 34g Sugar

INGREDIENTS:

For the Syrup:

- 1 cup sugar
- 1 cup water
- Juice of 1 lemon
- 1 tablespoon orange blossom water (optional)

For the Cake:

- 1 cup semolina
- 1/2 cup all-purpose flour
- 1/2 cup sugar
- 3 large eggs
- 1/2 cup plain yogurt
- 1/4 cup vegetable oil
- 1 teaspoon baking powder
- 1 teaspoon vanilla extract
- Zest of 1 lemon

DIRECTIONS:

Prepare the Syrup:

1. In a saucepan, combine sugar, water, and lemon juice. Bring to a boil, then simmer for 10 minutes until slightly thickened.
2. Stir in the orange blossom water if using, then set aside to cool completely.

Make the Cake:

1. Preheat your oven to 350°F (175°C). Grease an 8-inch square baking dish.
2. In a mixing bowl, whisk together the eggs and sugar until light and fluffy.
3. Add yogurt, oil, and vanilla extract. Mix until well combined.
4. In another bowl, combine semolina, flour, baking powder, and lemon zest. Gradually fold the dry ingredients into the wet mixture until a smooth batter forms.
5. Pour the batter into the prepared baking dish, spreading it evenly.
6. Bake for 25-30 minutes, or until the cake is golden brown and a toothpick inserted into the center comes out clean.
7. Once the cake is baked, remove it from the oven and let it cool for 5 minutes. Cut the cake into diamond or square shapes while still in the pan.
8. Pour the cooled syrup evenly over the warm cake, allowing it to soak in.
9. Let the cake rest for at least 2 hours to fully absorb the syrup.
10. Serve the cake at room temperature, optionally garnished with nuts like almonds or pistachios.

TIP: For an added touch of flavor and texture, sprinkle the top of the Revani with shredded coconut or finely chopped pistachios before serving. This not only enhances the presentation but also adds a delightful crunch that complements the moist cake.

Bougatza (Greek Custard Phyllo Pastry)

PREPARATION TIME: 20 MINUTES

COOKING TIME: 30 MINUTES

SERVES: 6-8

Nutrition Information (Per Serving):
320 Calories / 18g Fat / 36g Carbohydrates / 6g Protein / 160mg Sodium / 18g Sugar

INGREDIENTS:

For the Custard:
- 3 cups whole milk
- 1/2 cup fine semolina
- 1/2 cup sugar
- 3 large eggs
- 1 teaspoon vanilla extract
- Zest of 1 lemon
- 1/4 cup unsalted butter, melted

For the Pastry:
- 10 sheets phyllo dough
- 1/2 cup unsalted butter, melted (for brushing)

For Serving:
- Powdered sugar, for dusting
- Ground cinnamon, for dusting

DIRECTIONS:

Prepare the Custard:
1. In a medium saucepan, heat the milk over medium heat until it just begins to simmer.
2. Gradually whisk in the semolina and sugar, stirring constantly to prevent lumps. Cook for about 5-7 minutes until the mixture thickens.
3. Remove from heat and allow the mixture to cool slightly.
4. In a separate bowl, whisk the eggs, then slowly add them to the cooled semolina mixture, whisking constantly. Stir in the vanilla extract, lemon zest, and melted butter until smooth.
5. Set the custard aside to cool completely.

Assemble the Bougatza:
1. Preheat your oven to 350°F (175°C). Grease a 9x13-inch baking dish.
2. Lay a sheet of phyllo dough in the baking dish, allowing the edges to hang over the sides. Brush with melted butter.
3. Repeat with 5 more sheets, brushing each sheet with butter as you layer them.
4. Pour the cooled custard mixture over the phyllo layers and spread evenly.
5. Fold the overhanging edges of phyllo over the custard. Layer the remaining phyllo sheets on top, brushing each with butter.
6. Tuck the edges of the top layers into the sides of the dish.

Bake:
Bake in the preheated oven for 25-30 minutes or until the top is golden and crisp.

Serve:
1. Let the bougatza cool slightly, then cut it into squares.
2. Dust with powdered sugar and cinnamon before serving.

Cooking Measurements & Kitchen Conversions

Dry Measurements Conversion Chart

Teaspoons	Tablespoons	Cups
3 tsp	1 tbsp	1/16 c
6 tsp	2 tbsp	1/8 c
12 tsp	4 tbsp	1/4 c
24 tsp	8 tbsp	1/2 c
36 tsp	12 tbsp	3/4 c
48 tsp	16 tbsp	1 c

Liquid Measurements Conversion Chart

Fluid Ounces	Cups	Pints	Quarts	Gallons
8 fl.oz	1 c	1/2 pt	1/4 qt	1/16 gal
16 fl.oz	2 c	1 pt	1/2 qt	1/8 gal
32 fl.oz	4 c	2 pt	1 qt	1/4 gal
64 fl.oz	8 c	4 pt	2 qt	1/2 gal
128 fl.oz	16 c	8 pt	4 qt	1 gal

Liquid Measurements (Volume)

Standard	Metric
1/5 tsp	1 ml
1 tsp	5 ml
1 tbsp	15 ml
1 c (8 fl.oz)	240 ml
34 fl.oz	1 liter

Dry Measurements (Weight)

Standard	Metric
.035 oz	1 g
3.5 oz	100 g
17.7 oz (1.1 lb)	500 g
35 oz	1 kg

US to Metric Conversions

Standard	Metric
1/5 tsp	1 ml
1 tsp	5 ml
1 tbsp	15 ml
1 fl. oz	30 ml
1 c	237 ml
1 pt	473 ml
1 qt	.95 liter
1 gal	3.8 liters
1 oz	28 g
1 lb	454 g

Oven Temperatures Conversion

Fahrenheit	Celsius
250 °F	120 °C
320 °F	160 °C
350 °F	180 °C
375 °F	190 °C
400 °F	205 °C
425 °F	220 °C

1 Cup

1 cup = 8 fluid ounces
1 cup = 16 tablespoons
1 cup = 48 teaspoons
1 cup = 1/2 pint
1 cup = 1/4 quart
1 cup = 1/16 gallon
1 cup = 240 ml.

SHOPPING LIST

Creating a shopping list for the recipes in this book requires thoughtful planning to ensure you have all the essential ingredients. Below is a comprehensive shopping list that covers a wide range of items needed to prepare dishes in the "The Complete Mediterranean Diet Cookbook for Beginners". The list is organized by category to make your shopping trip as efficient as possible. Check your pantry for any staples you might already have. With a well-prepared list, you can enjoy a smooth, stress-free cooking experience. Additionally, consider buying fresh produce from local markets for the best quality and flavor. Taking time to plan ensures you have everything needed to create delicious Mediterranean meals with ease.

Fruit, Vegetables & Berries

- Artichokes
- Arugula
- Asparagus
- Avocados
- Banana
- Beets
- Bell Peppers
- Broccoli
- Brussels Spouts
- Cabbage
- Cantaloupe
- Carrots
- Cauliflower
- Celery
- Cherry Tomatoes
- Cucumbers
- Eggplant
- Figs
- Garlic Cloves
- Grapefruit
- Grapes
- Green Beans
- Green Onion
- Green Peas
- Kale
- Lemons
- Limes
- Mint
- Mix of Berries
- Mushrooms
- Olives
- Oranges
- Parsley
- Pomegranate Seeds
- Potatoes
- Red Onion
- Salad Mix
- Shallot
- Spinach Leaves
- Sweet Potatoes
- Tomatoes
- Watermelon

Herbs & Spices

- Aleppo Pepper
- Allspice
- Basil
- Bay Leaves
- Black Pepper
- Cilantro
- Cinnamon
- Cinnamon
- Cloves
- Coriander
- Cumin
- Dill
- Finely
- Garlic Powder
- Ground Ginger
- Mint Leaves
- Mustards Seeds
- Nutmeg
- Oregano
- Paprika
- Parsley
- Peppercorns
- Red Pepper Flakes
- Rosemary
- Saffron
- Salt
- Sumac
- Thyme
- Turmeric
- Za'atar

Dairy & Eggs

- Almond Milk
- Butter
- Butter (Unsalted)
- Coconut Milk
- Eggs
- Feta Cheese
- Goat Cheese
- Greek Yogurt
- Heavy Cream
- Mascarpone Cheese
- Milk
- Mozzarella Cheese
- Parmesan Cheese
- Planed Yogurt
- Ricotta Cheese
- Sour Cream

Grains & Legumes

- Baguette
- Black Beans
- Bulgur Wheat
- Chickpeas
- Couscous
- Currants
- Dried Cranberries
- Farro
- Granola
- Lasagna Noodles
- Lentils
- Medjool Dates
- Orzo Pasta
- Paella Rice
- Pasta
- Phyllo Dough
- Pita Bread
- Puff Pastry
- Quinoa
- Raisins
- Rice (Different Types)
- Rolled Oats
- Semolina Flour
- Sesame Seeds
- White Beans
- White Bread
- Whole Grain Bread
- Whole Wheat Tortillas

Nuts & Seeds

- Almonds
- Pine Nuts
- Pistachios
- Sesame Seeds
- Walnuts

Canned & Pantry Items

- Almond Extract
- Almond Flour
- Apple Cider Vinegar
- Balsamic Glaze
- Balsamic Vinegar
- Brewed Coffee
- Canned Black Beans
- Canned Chickpeas
- Canned Corn
- Canned Tomatoes
- Canned Tuna
- Canned White Beans
- Capers
- Chicken Broth
- Dijon Mustard
- Fish Broth
- Honey
- Jar of Grapes Leaves
- Kalamata Olives
- Lady Finger Cookies
- Lemon Juice
- Maple Syrup
- Marinara Sause
- Mayonnaise
- Olive Oil
- Orange Juice
- Red Wine
- Red Wine Vinegar
- Roasted Red Peppers
- Rose/Orange Water
- Sliced Black Olives
- Sun-dried Tomatoes
- Tarama (Fish Roe)
- Tomato Paste
- Tomato Sause
- Unflavored Gelatin
- Vanilla Extract
- Vegetable Broth
- White Wine
- Whole Wheat Flour

Meat & Poultry

- Beef Steak
- Beef Stew Meat

			Baking Supplies	Yeast
Beef Tenderloin	Sausages	Octopus	**Baking Supplies**	Yeast
Bone-in Pork Chops	Sirloin Steak	Salmon	All-Purpose Flour	**Other Items**
Chicken Breast	Turkey Breast	Sardines	Baking Powder	Aluminum Foil
Chicken Wings		Scallops	Baking Soda	Cooking Spray
Ground Beef	**Fish & Seafood**	Sea Bass	Cocoa Power	Kitchen Twine
Ground Lamb	Calamari Squid	Shrimp	Cornmeal	Metal Skewers
Lamb Chops	Cod	Swordfish Steaks	Cornstarch	Parchment Paper
Lamb Shanks	Haddock	Tilapia Fillets	Sugar	Toothpicks
Pork Tenderloin	Mussels	Tuna Steaks		Wooden Skewers

Please adjust the quantities based on the number of servings and your specific dietary preferences. Before heading to the store, double-check the recipes in the book to ensure you have everything you need, and feel free to add any additional items you may require for your personal needs or preferences. Don't forget to consider seasonal ingredients, which can enhance the flavor and freshness of your dishes. Planning your shopping trip in advance can also help you stay organized and reduce food waste.

Enjoy your culinary adventure—happy cooking!

GRATITUDE

Dear Customer,

Thank you for choosing **"The Complete Mediterranean Diet Cookbook for Beginners."** Your support means the world to me and my family. I'm truly grateful that you've welcomed this book into your kitchen. I hope these recipes inspire you to embrace the vibrant flavors, wholesome ingredients, and joyful spirit of Mediterranean cooking. Whether you're new to this lifestyle or looking to expand your culinary repertoire, I believe this book will help you create delicious, healthy meals that nourish both body and soul.

Cooking is more than just a daily task; it's an opportunity to connect with the people we love and the traditions we cherish. With this book, I hope to bring a bit of that warmth and connection into your home. I am honored that you've chosen to embark on this culinary journey with me, and I can't wait to hear about the memories you create around your table. Your trust in these recipes is a gift I don't take lightly, and I'm committed to making your cooking experience as enjoyable and rewarding as possible.

Thank you for being a part of this journey and for allowing me to be a part of yours.

With gratitude,

Myla Slobodian

Made in United States
Troutdale, OR
12/28/2024

27383787R00051